J. (James) Barmby

Gregory The Great

J. (James) Barmby

Gregory The Great

ISBN/EAN: 9783742828828

Manufactured in Europe, USA, Canada, Australia, Japa

Cover: Foto ©Thomas Meinert / pixelio.de

Manufactured and distributed by brebook publishing software (www.brebook.com)

J. (James) Barmby

Gregory The Great

The Fathers for English Readers.

GREGORY THE GREAT.

BY
REV. JAMES BARMBY, B.D.
VICAR OF PITTINGTON;
LATE PRINCIPAL OF BISHOP HATFIELD'S HALL, DURHAM;
AND FORMERLY FELLOW OF MAGDALEN COLLEGE, OXFORD.

PUBLISHED UNDER THE DIRECTION OF THE TRACT
COMMITTEE.

LONDON.
SOCIETY FOR PROMOTING CHRISTIAN KNOWLEDGE.
NORTHUMBERLAND AVENUE, CHARING CROSS;
4, ROYAL EXCHANGE; AND 48, PICCADILLY.

NEW YORK: POTT, YOUNG, & CO.
1879.

CONTENTS.

CHAPTER I.

Gregory and his Age—Ascendency of the Church—Results of Controversies—Imperial Domination—The Roman See—Effects of Barbarian Invasions—Justinian—Pope Vigilius—The Three Chapters—Spread of Christianity—Jurisdiction of the Popes—Monasticism—Benedict of Nursia—State of Morals and Religion *page* 9

CHAPTER II.

Gregory's Parentage, Education, Early Life—He becomes a Monk—Ordination and Residence at Constantinople—Return to Monastic Life—Asceticism—Distressed state of Italy—Election to the Popedom—Reluctance to accept—Gregory as Pope—Habits of Life—Istrian Bishops—Deference to the Emperor—African Donatists—Sanction of Persecution—Tolerance towards Jews (540-591) . . . . *page* 29

CHAPTER III.

Correction of Monastic Abuses—Separation of Monks and Clergy—Exemption of Monasteries from Episcopal Control—Case of Venantius—Nunneries—Sanctity of Marriage—Endowments—Election of Bishops—Confirmation—Use of the Pall—Respect for Episcopal Rights—Januarius of Cagliari—Natalis of Salona—Correction of Clerks—Sanctuary—Privileges of Clergy—Celibacy—Administration of the Patrimony—Charities . . . . *page* 52

CHAPTER IV.

The Church in Spain—Letters to Leander and Reccared—Appeal of two Spanish Bishops to Rome—Correspondence with Irish Bishops—St. Columban's Letters—Eastern Illyricum—Hadrianus—Natalis—Maximus—Remonstrance with the Emperor—Letter to the Empress—Final settlement—Claim to authority over the Eastern Church—Letter to John the Faster—Lombard Invasion—Gregory's Sermons—Patriotic activity—Thwarted by the Exarch—Letters to the Emperor and Empress—Truce with the Lombards—John the Faster calls himself Universal Bishop—Gregory's view of the question—His remonstrances—His sarcastic vein—He addresses the Patriarchs of Antioch and Alexandria—Cyriacus succeeds John the Faster—Gregory's renewed remonstrance—Correspondence with the Patriarchs—His view of St. Peter's Primacy being shared by Antioch and Alexandria—Renewed Lombard invasions—Gregory's activity—Results of his efforts (591-596) . *page* 71

CHAPTER V.

The Mission to England—Story of the Slaves in the Roman Forum—State of the Church in France—Correspondence with Brunehild—Pall sent to Virgilius—Reforms urged—Candidus sent—Cyriacus—A General Synod desired—Failure to obtain one—Eventual results—Augustine despatched to England—His success—His alleged Miracles—His questions and the replies to them—Scheme for the English Church—Letter to Mellitus—Letters to Bertha and Ethelbert—The British Christians—The Lombards—Theodelinda—Conversion of Agilulph (596–601) . . . . . . *page* 104

CHAPTER VI.

Accession of Phocas—His Character—His treatment of Mauricius and the Imperial family—Gregory's letters to him—To Leontia—Consideration of Gregory's conduct on this occasion—Its result—Former letters in praise of Mauricius — Palliations — Suffering from gout — Last letter to Theodelinda—Death and burial—Conduct of the mob after his death—Archdeacon Peter—Personal appearance of Gregory—His costume—Ecclesiastical Vestments in his day—Relics of him preserved at Rome (601–606) . . . . *page* 130

CHAPTER VII.

Gregory's writings—His letters — Extracts from them: To the Subdeacon Peter—To Marinianus of Ravenna—To Dominicus of Centumcellæ—To Maximus of Salona—To the ex-Prefect Libertinus—To Gregoria, a lady at Court—To the Emperor's sister, Theoctista—Another letter to the same lady—Liber Pastoralis Curæ—Its renown—Its plan—Summary of its contents—The Book of Dialogues—Occasion of its composition—Its contents—References to Benedict of Nursia—the fourth book about the state of the soul after death—Its effects on Christian thought—Commentary on Job—Milman's account of it—Specimens of its style—Homilies—On Ezekiel—On the Gospels— Extracts— Sacramentary, Antiphonary Hymns — The Lord's Prayer in the Eucharistic Office—Genuineness and style of the Hymns—Gregorian and Ambrosian music . . *page* 144

CHAPTER VIII.

Gregory's character—His talents—His attainments—His doctrinal views—On the authority of the Church—Augustinianism—Baptism—The Eucharist—Purgatory—Intercession of Saints—Relics—Pictures and Images—Slavery—Authority of the Roman See—Results of his policy . . . . *page* 191

GREGORY THE GREAT.

CHAPTER I.

Gregory and his Age—Ascendency of the Church—Results of Controversies—Imperial Domination—The Roman See—Effects of Barbarian Invasions—Justinian—Pope Vigilius—The Three Chapters—Spread of Christianity—Jurisdiction of the Popes—Monasticism—Benedict of Nursia—State of Morals and Religion.

If the title "Great," applied to an historical personage, may be rightly defined as implying the combination of high moral purpose with commanding ability, so used as to affect extensively the history of mankind, such title has not been without cause assigned to the first Pope Gregory. In all cases favourable circumstances are of course required, that the result may be actual, not mere potential, greatness. There must be suitable environments for the development and display of all high and influential life. Gregory might have lived and died with no renown beyond that of ascetic saintliness, had not circumstances called him when they did from his monastery to the highest seat in Christendom; and even there in a less eventful age his great qualities might not have found their adequate field for exercise. He stands out on the page of history as a striking instance of a remarkable man, at a remarkable time, being placed by Providence in a position peculiarly suitable for the exercise of his powers. The position was not of his own seeking; he shrank from it; he would fain have declined it altogether; greatness, in the sense of great estate, was "thrust upon" him; but, when it came, he showed himself at once worthy of it. And it is to be observed, that, though he sought it not, yet in one sense he himself "achieved" it, inasmuch as it was his acknowledged and peculiar fitness that caused all concerned in his elevation to force its acceptance upon him.

A brief preliminary sketch of the position of the Church, and especially of the Roman see, in relation to the world at the time of St. Gregory's accession, and of the causes that had led up to the existing state of things, will assist our understanding of his field of work.

At the close of the sixth century, when the first Gregory became pope, Paganism had long virtually disappeared from the Roman Empire; it was no longer a power to be considered, though it still lingered extensively, especially in country places, in spite of repression; Christianity was everywhere maintained and dominant. The emperors too, whether orthodox or heretical, had long taken a warm interest in church affairs, had summoned councils, promulgated and enforced their decrees; and, however morally corrupt society in high places might be, its atmosphere had been impregnated with theology. The result had been, among other things, a large advance in the importance of the hierarchy, and especially of the great patriarchal sees; but at the same time (in the East at least) increasing subservience to the imperial power, which, while treating prelates with much external respect, had been in the habit of dictating to them in fact, commanding their elevation or deposition, and at times trenching more or less even on their spiritual prerogatives by assuming to itself a kind of priestly power.

The controversies that had been the peculiar feature of Church history in the preceding centuries had furthered these results. The need felt for centres of unity and support against the aggressions of heretical speculation; the importance accruing to bishops, and especially to metropolitans and patriarchs, to whom in synod and general council the definition of the faith had been consigned, had enhanced the dignity of the episcopal order, while, on the other hand, the somewhat imperious attitude of the emperors in connection with such controversies and councils,—the latter being convened by their sole authority, controlled by them during their sittings, and dependent on them for ratification and the enforcement of their decrees,—had at the same time advanced imperialism. And, further, however important for all future time were the dogmatic decisions of that age of conflict, its immediate effects were likely to be demoralizing, as they certainly were replete with ill blood and discord. When the leaders of the Church had so long been habitually occupied in bitter controversy, dealing anathemas against each other, deposing and being deposed, their very councils often scenes of violence; when Christian communities were divided into parties, often fighting to bloodshed for rival tenets, or in support of rival bishops; when salvation had come to be regarded as dependent on accurate definitions of nice points of mysterious doctrine far more than on charity or holiness of life;—the effects were necessarily disastrous to the peace and morality of the Church at large. It is to be observed, however, that throughout the period referred to the see of Rome had occupied a peculiar position, and been much less affected either by imperial domination or by doctrinal conflict than the patriarchates of the East. The tendency of events had been in fact to aggrandise exceptionally, and give a sort of sacred lustre to, the occupants of St. Peter's chair. With regard to the great controversies that had so embittered and divided the Church, the West had been comparatively free from them, and the popes had taken but little part in them; but they had with one or two temporary exceptions supported uniformly the cause of orthodoxy; they had countenanced and protected orthodox prelates who had fled to them under persecution; they had been represented, though not present, in all the general councils held in the East to define the faith, and had ratified their decrees; they had often been able to defy emperors who favoured heresy with a spirit and success little known in the more subservient East, and thus advancing their claims to be, as St. Peter's successors, the unfailing guardians of Apostolical tradition, and assumed a headship over all the Churches, which though by no means universally acknowledged, had gained extensive credence.

THE GROWTH OF THE PAPAL CLAIMS.

Political events had also favoured the independence and influence of the Roman see. The removal of the seat of empire from Rome to Constantinople by Constantine had, from the very commencement of the State's acknowledgment of Christianity, left the bishops of the old city free from the depressing domination of a court from which their Eastern rivals continually suffered. Freedom was further secured, during the periods when there was a Western as well as an Eastern emperor, by the removal of the residence of the former under Honorius (A.D. 404) to Ravenna. Rome itself had, indeed, long before this removal ceased to be the usual residence of the emperors. Since the beginning of the reign of Diocletian (277) they had held their court at Milan.

In such circumstances the importance of the popes had, since the time of Constantine, gone on increasing; to their acknowledged spiritual position as the occupants of the first see in Christendom, the representatives of St. Peter, the sole great patriarchs of the West, was added a temporal position of no mean importance. As the most influential potentates in the ancient imperial city, supported by the spiritual allegiance of the West, they had been enabled, though still subjects of the emperors, to hold their own against them in ecclesiastical matters with success, and were a power which had to be counted on by the State.

The invasions of the Roman empire by barbarian hordes, which had been the most important historical event of a century or two before the time of Gregory, being destined to found a new Europe on the ruins of old Roman civilization, had further strengthened the Papal power, and opened the way for its development. The most memorable of these invasions,—those which resulted in the capture of Rome itself,—had been confronted by popes of singular eminence, who more than any others asserted and advanced the prerogatives of the Holy See.

Innocent I. was pope when (A.D. 410) Rome fell into the hands of Alaric the Goth; Leo the Great when Attila the Hun (452) and Genseric the Vandal (455) were the successive conquerors. Each event, however notoriously disastrous, left the Church, and the see of Rome, in a higher position than before. The first accomplished the breaking up and dispersion of the old Roman families which had been the props of ancient heathenism, and the demolition of the ancient temples, afterwards left in ruins or converted into churches; it was regarded as a divine judgment on old heathen, rather than on Christian, Rome, especially as the Gothic invaders, being Christians though Arians, had singularly respected places and persons of Christian sanctity: and Innocent, who had been providentially absent (not through cowardice, but on a mission of duty,) during the siege and capture, when he returned to the city after the departure of the invaders, found himself in a position of singular eminence. He was henceforth without rival the greatest man in Rome; the head and organizer of a new Christian Rome rising out of the ruins of devastated heathen Rome; both his character and his conduct during the crisis, and his position afterwards, enhanced his prestige and his power in proportion as those of the weak emperor

Honorius, timidly inefficient at Ravenna, had decayed. Then, when Attila with his heathen Huns seemed to have Italy and Rome at his feet, it had been neither emperor nor general, but Pope Leo to whom the sole glory had accrued of checking him in his career of conquest, and, apparently in a great measure through a feeling of superstitious awe, inducing him to retire. And when, soon afterwards, the Arian Vandal Genseric devastated Rome, it was the same great pope who alone obtained some mitigation of the horrors of the conquest; and when that storm too had passed away, it left the Western Empire wounded to the death, but the see of Rome with its prestige and its lustre unimpaired.

Only fifteen years after the death of Pope Leo, the Western Empire expired in Augustulus, and the Herulian Odoacer, and after him Theodoric the Ostrogoth, both Arian Christians, became rulers in the West. Under such rule it might have been expected that the head of Western Catholicity would suffer an eclipse. But it was not so. These princes were peculiarly tolerant, treated the Catholic clergy, and especially the pope, with respect, and in no way evinced any desire to interfere in Church affairs, except, when called upon, to rectify flagrant abuses attending elections to the popedom. Under this rule it was that Felix III., and his successors for more than forty years, had been able to defy emperors and patriarchs, in the matter of Acacius, and to renounce communion with the whole Eastern Church. Under the same rule Pope Hormisdas had at length dictated his own terms of communion to the East, and, with the aid of the orthodox Emperor Justin, ended the schism in a way that was, on the whole, a striking triumph to the Apostolic See.

The reconquest of Italy for Justinian by Belisarius (536) had, however, brought about a change in the relation of the popes to the State, and been followed, in fact, by a period of unusual humiliation to the papal chair. Religious zeal in high places, combined with principles of oriental despotism, soon proved a bad exchange for the indifference or the tolerance of the Arian ruler. The Eastern emperors had long been accustomed to ecclesiastical domination over the patriarchs and prelates in their own domain,— domination the more humiliating for the female influence and court intrigues that too often were elements in its exercise,—and the bishops of Rome were now to be in like manner treated as vassals. The story is well known of the reigning pope, Silverius, after the entry of Belisarius into Rome, being peremptorily summoned to the bedchamber of Antonina, the wife of the general, and the confidante of the Empress Theodora, who, sitting on her bed with her husband at her feet, ordered then and there his deposition and banishment. It is well known too how, after this, Vigilius was, by command of Theodora, uncanonically made pope by Belisarius, on the understanding that, in return for his elevation and for a large bribe received, he should profess the Monophysite creed, which that empress favoured. In these transactions Justinian himself was not personally concerned; but the very fact that they could take place without his cognizance shows only the more clearly to what degradation the immediate supremacy of a corrupt court might reduce the Church. He, however, in his own orthodox way, was also arbitrary enough, and, to whatever extent his legislation might benefit the clergy, he had no idea of even popes resisting his imperial will: especially as he himself prided himself on being a theologian. Having issued in 544, on his own authority, an edict condemning as heretical the writings (called the Three Chapters) of three deceased prelates, Theodore of Mopsuesta, Theodoret, and Ibas (though the two last had been expressly acquitted of heresy by the Council of Chalcedon), he peremptorily summoned to Constantinople Vigilius, who, along with the bishops of the West, had refused to join in the condemnation. Thrice, under pressure and contumelious usage, the unhappy pope complied, and thrice recanted. The fifth Œcumenical Council (553) which, under the emperor's dictation, condemned the three Chapters, he not only refused to attend, but also issued a defence of the writings condemned; but afterwards, in spite of his protest, accepted its decrees. He cut but a sorry figure throughout: his commencement was disgraceful; he wavered between independence and subservience during his subsequent career. His successor Pelagius, though he had previously with Vigilius defended the three Chapters, also assented after his accession to their condemnation; for which assent his authority was repudiated by several Western Churches. Between Pelagius and Gregory came the three popes, John III., Benedict I., and Pelagius II., whose reigns were singularly obscure and uneventful. The blight of imperialism at this time dimmed the lustre of the great Roman see. Events had, however, in the meantime occurred which, while they greatly increased, in many respects, the difficulties of Gregory's position, at any rate had again relieved his see from the pressure of imperial despotism. The Lombards had already crossed the Alps and gained possession of Northern Italy: at the time of Gregory's accession they threatened Rome, while the Emperor at Constantinople was cowed and powerless. None of the barbarian invaders of Italy have been painted by their contemporaries in such black colours as the Lombards. Their invasion was worse than that even of the hideous heathen Huns; for it was not merely that of a savage army that came and departed; it was the migration of a savage people, with their wives and families, taking savage possession of the country. Arians like the Goths, they do not appear to have had their reverence for Christian sanctities. They are said to have destroyed churches, violated virgins, spread round them devastation and terror. There may be exaggeration by the writers of the time, actuated by fear and indignation, of the enormities of their character and conduct; but such is the picture given of them. It was mainly the misery and the disorganization caused by them to which we may probably attribute the then prevalent belief, often expressed by Gregory himself, that the end of all things was approaching: it was the panic and desperation induced by their approach that caused all classes at Rome, recognizing in their need the character of Gregory, to fix on him as the only man for steering the bark of St. Peter through the storm.

Such was the political state of things when St. Gregory took the helm—a state of things of especial importance in this respect, that now was the period of transition from the old order to the new; from the Church under the wing of the old Roman Empire christianized, to the Church exercising independent sway from Rome over nations of new blood and new institutions which were forming themselves throughout Europe; from imperialism to the mediæval papacy. Gregory lived at a critical time in this eventful period; a time when the Western empire had just expired and the Eastern was languishing; and when the new nations were notably gaining power and position; and it was, humanly speaking, due especially to him that the system of papal monarchy, already contemplated and prepared for by an Innocent and a Leo, took definite and lasting form.

At this time many of the Teutonic nations who were destined to constitute Christian Europe had already been more or less converted; but all except the Franks had at first or subsequently adopted Arianism. This important exception was due to Clovis, king of the Salian Franks, influenced by his queen, Clotilda (a Catholic Burgundian princess), and by a vow made at the battle of Tolbiacum (Zülpich, A.D. 496), having adopted Catholicism (being baptized by St. Remigius, bishop of Rheims), and having been followed by his subjects. Afterwards, owing partly to the example and influence of this preponderating race, others had also professed orthodoxy: the Burgundians, under their king, Sigismund (517); the Suevi, under their kings, Carrarich (550-559) and

Theodemir (559–569); the Visigoths in Spain, under their king, Reccared, at the Council of Toledo (589). Since the Ostrogothic kingdom in Upper Italy, and the Vandalic in Western Africa, had been destroyed under Justinian, Arianism had also lost its hold in these territories. But the terrible Lombards, who now occupied a great part of Northern Italy and threatened the South, were still Arians. Even there, however, it was not long before Catholicity obtained a footing, through the influence of a Catholic queen, as will be seen hereafter. Orthodox churches existed in Britain and Ireland, though in Britain now driven, since the Saxon invasion (449), into the mountains of Wales, Cornwall, and the north of the island.

With regard to the authority of the Bishop of Rome—when St. Gregory took the reins—claimed or acknowledged, over the above-mentioned and other parts of the Christian world, it was of three kinds:—1st, episcopal; 2ndly, metropolitan; 3rdly, patriarchal. His episcopate comprised only the city of Rome; as metropolitan he had oversight of the seven suffragan, afterwards called cardinal, bishops of the Roman territory, those of Ostia, Portus, Silva Candida, Sabina, Præneste, Tusculum, and Albanum; his patriarchate seems to have originally extended (according to Rufinus, the ecclesiastical historian, writing towards the end of the fourth century) over the suburban provinces which were under the civil jurisdiction of the *vicarius urbis*, including Upper Italy, with the islands of Sicily, Sardinia, and Corsica. But being the only patriarch in the West, he had in fact claimed and exercised jurisdiction as such beyond these original limits, including in this way all the four vicariates into which the præfecture of Italy was politically divided; not that of Rome only, but those also of Northern Italy, with its centre at Milan, Western Illyricum, with its capital at Sirmium, and Western Africa, with its capital at Carthage. In the last-named region the popes had indeed in past times (notably in the time of Cyprian) succeeded very imperfectly in their assertions of authority; but after the oppressive domination of the Arian Vandals, the Catholics there, delivered by Justinian's conquest, A.D. 534, readily admitted the spiritual suzerainty of Rome. Eastern Illyricum too, though annexed by the Emperor Gratian (379), when he divided Illyria, to the Eastern Empire, having during the Arian disputes belonged to the Western, and having been faithful to the Nicene faith, had, after the separation, turned itself to Rome rather than to Constantinople; and the popes Damasus and Siricius had taken advantage of the opportunity to assign to the bishops of Thessalonica patriarchal jurisdiction over the new præfecture as vicars of the Roman see. And this relation of East Illyria to Rome had become afterwards an accomplished fact. In Gaul also, while still under imperial rule, the popes had long exercised spiritual authority. Disputes having arisen between the bishops of Arles and Vienne, Pope Zozimus had, as early as A.D. 417, assigned metropolitan rights to the former, making the bishop of Arles vicar of the Apostolic See, as the bishop of Thessalonica had been made in Illyria. Subsequent popes had maintained this arrangement, though not always without resistance on the part of the Gallican bishops. Further, beyond any limits that can be definitely assigned, the influence of the bishops of Rome extended. At whatever date their claim to a sort of jurisdiction over the whole Church Catholic, as successors of the Prince of the Apostles, began, and however unknown such authority might be in more primitive times, the claim had long been made. Synodical decrees and imperial edicts had been used to support such extended jurisdiction. The Western council of Sardica (347) had accorded to the then pope, Julius, the power of sending judges to hear on the spot the appeals of condemned bishops, at any rate throughout the West; and the successors of Julius had quoted the canons of this council erroneously as those of Nice, and as empowering the popes in perpetuity to summon cases from all parts to be heard at Rome. Further, during the ecclesiastical disputes in Gaul about the jurisdiction of Arles in the time of Pope Leo I., the Emperor Valentinian had made a law constituting the pope supreme head of the whole Western Church, with power to summon bishops from all parts to abide his judgments. In the East (except in the case of bishops courting the support of Rome against oppression) such claims had indeed been ever resisted, but even there the pre-eminence, as distinct from the jurisdiction, of the see of old Rome, was recognized. And elsewhere, though with varying degrees of independence, the barbaric conquerors of Europe naturally regarded with peculiar reverence the prelate of the old Eternal City, the one great Western patriarch, the representative (as they had been taught) of the Prince of the

Apostles, to whom the keys of the kingdom of heaven had been committed. With what watchfulness and judgment Gregory cultivated, as he had opportunity, the ground thus being prepared for the future harvest, as well as reformed and consolidated the part of the Church already under his fuller sway, will appear as his life goes on.

For an understanding of the religious tone of the age of Gregory, as well as that of his own character, the rise and prevalence of monasticism must be taken into account. The system, having been introduced in the fourth century from the East, which was its original home, into the West, and having been encouraged and upheld from its outset by such distinguished men as St. Athanasius, St. Jerome, St. Ambrose, and St. Augustine, soon made extraordinary progress through the whole of Western Christendom, and had become universally recognized as that of the highest Christian life. While it had doubtless afforded scope for many saintly aspirations for which the turmoil and vices of ordinary society were often too little favourable, it had also fostered much fanaticism and credulity. It had withdrawn from direct service to their fellow-men hosts of devotees, who saw the only sure road to heaven in seclusion, excessive fasting, and self-inflicted pain, and who often proved themselves capable of wild fanatical violence; it had peopled the deserts, in the imagination of men, with miraculous visitations, ministering angels, and multitudes of assaulting devils; it had also encouraged a number of roving idlers, who covered idleness and sometimes sensuality with the cloak of saintliness;

but, on the other hand, it had offered to many a field for purity and undisturbed devotion, combined in many cases with manual industry and charitable deeds ; and it had impressed the corrupt society of the age with the sense of there being higher aims for man than eating and drinking, worldly ambition and enjoyment.

A new impulse and form had now been quite recently given to the system by Benedict of Nursia (born 480), who, by way of reforming the abuses and disorder into which it had fallen, had founded the great Benedictine order, and established (A.D. 529) his famous Monastery on Monte Cassino. The principles of monasticism, and the influence of this great reformer, had taken deep hold on the mind of Gregory, affecting his whole character and modes of thought. The first monk who had ascended the papal chair, he remained one in heart throughout his life; while, both in his actions and his writings, he did much towards advancing the system, and especially towards giving a fixed and permanent form to the conceptions about the spiritual world—the mythology (so to speak) of mediæval Christendom—which, springing mainly from the imaginations and visions of secluded enthusiasts, passed into the general creed of men.

With regard to the general moral condition of Christian society, it is usual, and not without reason, to represent it very unfavourably. The grossly corrupt civilization of the Roman empire had undoubtedly been an unpropitious field for the ameliorating influences of Christianity. The records of the preceding centuries of Christian imperialism leave on the mind a painful impression of religion taking the form of violent zeal for rival tenets rather than of charity and holiness; of vice and cruelty in Christian emperors and their surroundings; of intrigue and corruption in high places; of ambitious and violent prelates; of bloody conflicts between rival religious parties; of general corruption and disorder. The picture is not relieved when we turn to what is told us of the barbaric nations who had received the Gospel. There, however, it was not to be expected that its softening and sanctifying influences would be immediate or rapid; and we may be less surprised in reading of prevalent immorality and violence.

Of the monks, too, the theory of whose vocation was the attainment of a higher sanctity, and many of whom had doubtless taken to seclusion as a refuge from prevailing evils,—of them, too, we hear at times no flattering account from contemporary writers. We find evidence on the one hand of wild fanaticism, on the other (in the West especially) of indolence and mendicancy. The frequent decrees of synods against monastic irregularities are in themselves signs of a state of things that called for continual correction; and it was, in fact, the disorganization of the system that caused St. Benedict to attempt reform by the introduction of his rule, which provided, among other things, for a year's probation of novices, for continuance under regular discipline of such as were finally admitted, and the division of their time into fixed periods for devotion, study, and labour. The tone of some monastic communities before his reform may be gathered from an incident of his earlier life. While living as a hermit, he was invited by some neighbouring monks whose abbacy was vacant to accept the post. He did so after warning them that he would not be able to endure their manners; but before long returned to his solitude on finding that, offended by his strictness, they were attempting to poison him.

Those, however, draw a hasty and erroneous conclusion who, from the generally black colours of the picture presented to us by the records of the time, would infer the absence of true Christian life from either the cloister or society at large. Common history deals with striking and prominent events, with characters and acts that come to the top and make a noise in their day; and these, in times of conflict and disorganization, are apt to be of the violent, and often atrocious order. The quiet, unobtrusive virtues, those which it is the peculiar function of the Gospel to foster and to invest with dignity, may all the time be flourishing beneath the unobtrusive surface, and doing their silent work. History, occupied with more stirring topics, may pass them by; they lie outside the scope of satirists; divines, " vexed with the filthy conversation of the wicked," and intent on reproving sin, may depreciate them in their day, or leave scant notice of them in their writings; such evidences of them as do remain in the contemporary literature that has come down may not be perceived by ordinary readers, struck more by the eventful and the thrilling: but that the principles of a genuine

Christianity were by no means so rare as has been sometimes supposed; that the dews of grace watered many a region, fruitful of piety and active charity, protesting against, rebuking, and mitigating the evils of the time, may be concluded, not only from such principles being openly preached and acknowledged by all in theory, but also from notices that have been preserved of saintly persons and saintly deeds. St. Benedict was not the first monk of his age who had striven after holiness; he could not have gained the influence he did, had he not represented a class of devotees with aspirations corresponding to his own. St. Gregory and his family, which seems to have consisted of excellent Christians, were but specimens of what probably existed more widely than has been by some supposed, though he himself, through his talents and opportunities, towered above his age. His correspondence also shows that there were not a few who sympathized with him in his genuine piety, and responded to his appeals to their charity. And, again, with respect to the Christian nations of barbaric origin, it may be observed that even Gibbon, little inclined in general to overrate the benefits of the Gospel, owns its effects for good upon them, both in softening their existing barbarism, and in being pregnant with results in the future.[1]

Nor can we contemplate the zealous and successful work of missionaries among these nations without recognizing large wells of living water in the churches that sent them forth. So much it has seemed true

---

[1] Gibbon's "Decline and Fall," iv. p. 418.

and just to say with regard to the religion and morality of the age preceding that of Gregory and that in which he worked, which there may have been a tendency in some quarters to depreciate unduly. Whether or not the religion of the period wore in all respects the complexion which we in our day most approve—whether or not it was tinged with error, credulity, and superstition—is not the question that has been before us. Genuine faith and genuine religion may at times assume distorted or even grotesque forms : the things themselves retain their true nature in spite of form.

CHAPTER II.

Gregory's Parentage, Education, Early Life—He becomes a Monk—Ordination and Residence at Constantinople—Return to Monastic life—Asceticism—Distressed state of Italy—Election to the Popedom—Reluctance to accept—Gregory as Pope—Habits of life—Istrian Bishops—Deference to the Emperor—African Donatists—Sanction of persecution—Tolerance towards Jews (540—591).

THE exact date of Gregory's birth is unknown. It was probably about the year 540, some ten years after Benedict of Nursia had founded the Benedictine order. He was well-born, and well-educated. His father Gordianus was a wealthy Roman of senatorial rank, descended from a pope Felix (probably Felix III., who became pope A.D. 467), and described as a religious man. He bore the title "Regionarius," denoting an office of dignity, the precise nature of which is not clear. His mother Silvia (who, after her husband's death, lived in ascetic seclusion), and two sisters of Gordianus, Tarsilla and Æmiliana (who lived in their own house as dedicated virgins), have obtained a place in the calendar of Saints.[1] With such sur-

[1] "*Homilies on the Gospels:*" *Hom.* 38. It appears from this homily that Gregory's father, Gordianus, had three sisters, Æmiliana, Tarsilla, and Gordiana, all of whom had been dedicated virgins (not in a convent, but, as was customary among noble ladies, in a house of their own), but the last of whom, having no vocation, returned to the world. She had long been a source of grave anxiety to her pious sisters; she delighted in

roundings his early training is spoken of by John the Deacon, his biographer, as having been that of a saint among saints, and at no time of his life do his first religious impressions appear to have lost their hold on him. It is interesting to be able to form an idea of the outward aspect of parents under whose eye and influence such men as St. Gregory have grown up. We are enabled to do this in the present case through a description by John the Deacon of portraits of Gordianus and Silvia placed by their son, when pope, in his monastery of St. Andrew. The father is tall, has a long face, a grave countenance, "green" eyes, a moderate beard, and thick hair. The mother's face is round and fair, showing traces of great beauty though wrinkled with age; her countenance is cheerful, her eyes large and blue, and her lips comely. The description gives us the idea of an interesting pair, the more so from the contrast between them; and that of the mother especially of a very pleasant saint. It is further interesting to learn, from the same authority, that Gregory himself, who left his own portrait in the same monastery, combined the paternal

---

the society of worldly girls, and found the conversation of others wearisome. When her sisters lectured her, she would all at once assume a grave countenance, which only lasted till they had done, when she would return to her usual light discourse. The two saintly ones having died after having been favoured with visions, a delicious fragrance having surrounded the deathbed of one of them, and the knees of the other having been found after death as hard as a camel's from constant kneeling in prayer,—the unimpressible Gordiana, "forgetful of the fear of God, forgetful of shame and reverence, forgetful of her consecration," married the tenant of her lands.

and maternal features, his face being a happy medium between the length of his father's and the roundness of his mother's, "Most becomingly prolonged, with a certain rotundity." He had the advantage also of a liberal as well as a religious education, by which he profited so much that the historian Gregory of Tours, his contemporary, states that in grammar, rhetoric, and logic, he was considered second to none in Rome. He also studied law, as befitted his rank in life; he soon distinguished himself in the Senate; and, at an unusually early age (certainly before 573, in which year he would be little more than 30 years of age), he was appointed by the Emperor Justin II. to the dignified office of prætor of the city. While thus living in the world, pursuing honourably the career opened to him by his birth and talents, we find no allusion to any failure in purity of life; nor, on the other hand, to any ascetic affectation. He dressed, at any rate, conformably to his rank; for Gregory of Tours speaks of the contrast, striking the eyes of observers, between the monkish garb which he afterwards assumed and the silk attire, the sparkling gems, and the purple-striped trabea with which in the earlier period he had paced the streets of Rome. This mode of life, however, did not long satisfy his religious aspirations. We do not read in his case of any crisis of conversion, as in the case of some saints. As far as we know, he was always religious, having striven, while living in the world (as he says in one of his letters), to live to God also, but having found it difficult. Accordingly, on his father's death (the date of which is not known), he kept but a small part of the large patrimony that came to him, employing the rest in charitable uses, and especially in founding monasteries, of which he endowed six in Sicily, and one, dedicated to St. Andrew, on the site of his own house near the church of St. John and St. Paul at Rome, in which he himself became a monk. This was the line to which strong devotion would almost necessarily lead him at the age in which he lived, especially with the recent example of St. Benedict before him, whom he much admired, and of whom he has left us many interesting records.

With what fervency, or even excess, of zeal he took up the monastic life will appear presently. It was, however, soon interrupted by the pope, Benedict I., who required his services in the capacity of his representative (*apocrisiarius*) at Constantinople, to qualify him for which office, having summoned him from his monastery, he ordained him one of the seven deacons of Rome. Pelagius II. also employed him afterwards in the same capacity, requiring his services especially for urging on the emperor the necessity of sending aid to Rome, both in money and soldiers, against the aggressions of the Lombards, which the exarch at Ravenna had declared himself powerless to oppose. Gregory remained thus employed for several years at Constantinople; and the time so spent, however uncongenial to him the employment might be, was doubtless of great importance in preparing him for the high position to which he was afterwards to be called, bringing him in contact with the emperor and his court, giving him acquaintance with political parties and influences, and opportunity for cultivating the talent for diplomacy which he possessed in an eminent degree.

Secular affairs, however, did not occupy him entirely. We are told by his biographer, John the Deacon, that he found continual refuge from them in the society of many of his brother monks, who, out of their love to him, had followed him from Rome, and with whom he kept up his aspirations after the heavenly life, "retiring to their society from the constant storm of business as to a safe port, bound by their example, as by an anchor-cable, to the placid shore of prayer." He also found opportunity for the exercise of his theological acquirements. We find him engaged in a long dispute with the Constantinopolitan patriarch Eutychius, who had written a treatise on the nature of the body after the resurrection, maintaining that it would be of an impalpable kind, subtle as air. This position Gregory opposed, alleging the recorded palpability of the risen body of the Saviour, the first-fruit of the resurrection, which was such as could be touched and handled. The emperor himself, Tiberius, is said to have terminated the dispute in favour of Gregory; and both the disputants are affirmed to have been so fatigued by their controversy that they had both to take to their beds at its close. He also commenced during his stay—at the instigation (it is said) of Leander, Archbishop of Seville, whose intimate acquaintance he at this time formed—his famous commentary on the book of Job, of which further mention will be hereafter made. Recalled at length to Rome, he was allowed, at his own earnest request, to return to his monastery, of which he became the abbat on the removal of the former abbat Maximianus to the see of Syracuse; but was still employed by the pope as his secretary; and here he remained till, in the year 590, when he was about 50 years of age, circumstances again disturbed his peace, and forced the popedom upon him.

It has been said above that he threw himself with great zeal into monastic life. It appears from many passages in his writings to have been his ideal, not only of saintly perfection, but also of peaceful happiness. He says in his preface to his Dialogues, which were written (he tells us) by way of solace to his mind under the constant sadness arising from the cares of office: "My unhappy mind remembers what it was in the monastery; how it soared above the vicissitudes of fleeting things, because it thought only of things celestial; and, though retained in the body, transcended through contemplation the enclosures of the flesh; while even of death, which to almost all men appears a penalty, it was enamoured as being the entrance into life, and the reward of its labour. But now, by reason of the pastoral care, it has to bear with secular business, and, after so fair a vision of rest, is fouled by terrestrial dust. I ponder on what I now endure; I ponder on what I have lost. For lo! now I am shaken by the waves of a great sea, and in the ship of the mind am dashed by the storms of a strong tempest; and when I recall the condition of my former life, I sigh as one who sees with reverted eyes the shore that he has left behind." His asceticism appears to have been extreme, as was likely to be the case with a sincere devotee.

The monastic theory required it of all aspirants to perfection. His fasts are said to have been such as to endanger his life, had he not been induced to abate their rigour. He himself speaks in the Dialogues of his perpetual illnesses while in his convent, due probably (as might be also in part the bad health from which he suffered through life) to excessive abstinence. During one Holy Week it is particularly mentioned by his biographer that he fainted so frequently, and seemed so nearly at death's door, that he feared greatly lest he should not be able to continue his fast till Easter Day. But a holy monk, Eleutherius, from another convent, came and prayed for him that he might have strength to persevere; whereupon all at once he lost all desire for food, and even all recollection of his former craving, and, when Easter came, could have fasted a day longer, if he had wished to do so. We are told, further, that his mother Silvia, who at that time lived a secluded life in the neighbourhood, used to feed him in his monastery with raw peas or beans.[1] His regime as abbat may be judged of from an anecdote related by himself in his Dialogues,[2] which shall be given in his own words. It is introduced by him as evidence of the salutary effect of eucharistic offerings for the dead, and is interesting as also illustrating his tone of feeling and belief. "There was a certain monk called Justus, skilled in medicine, who had been accustomed to serve me diligently in the same monastery, and to

---

[1] "Life by John the Deacon," B. I. ch. vii. § ix.
[2] B. IV. ch. lv.

watch with me in my perpetual illnesses. He fell sick, and was reduced to the last stage. His own brother, Copiosus by name, who still practises medicine in this city, attended him. But the aforesaid Justus, when he perceived his end approaching, informed his brother Copiosus that he had three pieces of gold concealed. Which thing could not be hidden from the brethren, who, subtly searching, and examining his medicine, found the three gold pieces concealed in a drug. The matter being announced to me, I could not bear with equanimity so great an evil in a brother who had lived with us in common: for it had always been a rule of my monastery that the brethren should have everything in common, and no one anything of his own. Smitten then with excessive grief, I began to think what I should do either for the purgation of the dying man or for example to the living brethren. So I called to me Pretiosus, the prior of the monastery, and said: 'See that none of the brethren approach him as he is dying, and that he receive no word of consolation from any one's mouth; but when at the point of death he shall ask for the brethren, let his brother after the flesh tell him that on account of the hidden gold pieces he is abominated by them all; so that at least in death bitterness for his fault may pierce his soul, and purge him from the sin that he has committed. But after his death let not his body be laid with those of the brethren, but make a hole in any dunghill, and throw his body into it with the three gold pieces, all of you exclaiming together, "Thy money perish with thee"; and so cover him with earth.' All this was done, and had the effect I desired. For when this same monk was at the point of death, and anxiously desired to be commended to the brethren, and none of them deigned to come to him or speak to him, and when his brother after the flesh explained to him why he was abominated by them all, he groaned grievously for his sin, and in the midst of his sadness departed from this body, and was buried as I have said. But all the brethren, perturbed by this sentence upon him, began to bring forth even the commonest little things which they had been always allowed by the rule to have, being mightily afraid of keeping anything for which they might be blamed. But, when thirty days had elapsed, my mind began to commiserate the departed brother, and, thinking with deep sorrow of his punishments, to seek some way of delivering him. So I again summoned Pretiosus the prior, and said to him : 'It is now long that that brother who died has been tormented in fire : we ought to show him some charity, and further his deliverance as far as we can. Go, therefore, and see that the sacrifice be offered for him from this day daily for thirty days ; let no single day be omitted on which the salutary host is not offered for his absolution.' He departed, and obeyed. Now we, being otherwise occupied, did not keep count of the days as they passed by ; but on a certain night this departed brother appeared in a vision to his own brother Copiosus, to whose inquiry how he was he replied, 'Till now I have been in evil case, but now it is well with me ; for to-day I have received the communion.' Copiosus having at once informed the brethren in the monastery, they diligently computed the days, and found that it was the day on which the thirtieth oblation had been completed. And thus, as Copiosus had known nothing of what the brethren were doing for his brother, and as they had known nothing of what he had seen, the coincidence of the vision and the sacrifice proved clearly that the departed brother escaped punishment through the salutary host."

In this narration some modern readers may only see an unlovely union of inhumanity and superstition. But with regard to the charge of inhumanity it is to be borne in mind that Gregory was at the time in the fresh fervour of monastic enthusiasm. That he was really at heart both humane and charitable his subsequent life and letters prove. If he seems at first sight otherwise in this case, it was because a paramount religious motive had possession of him. And it is observable further, that all through the proceedings he had regard to the spiritual advantage of the offending monk quite as much as to the maintenance of the monastic rule. As to the superstition or credulity involved in the latter part of the story, more will be said hereafter about his mental attitude in these respects. All we need say here is that he held the views of his day. It is to be remembered also that he was not so absorbed in the contemplative life as to be incapable of an influx of missionary enthusiasm. For it was during this period that, roused by the sight of the English slaves in the market-place of Rome, he conceived the idea of going forth to convert England, of which more will be said hereafter.

Pope Pelagius died on the 8th of February, 590.

The people of Rome, as has been already intimated, were at this time in the utmost straits. Italy lay prostrate and miserable under the Lombard invasion; the invaders now threatened Rome itself, and its inhabitants trembled; famine and pestilence within the city produced a climax of distress; an overflow of the Tiber at the time aggravated the general alarm and misery; Gregory himself, in one of his letters, compares Rome at this time to an old and shattered ship, letting in the waves on all sides, tossed by a daily storm, its planks rotten and sounding of wreck.

In this state of things all men's thoughts at once turned to Gregory. The pope was at this period the virtual ruler of Rome, and the greatest power in Italy; and they must have Gregory as their pope; for, if any one could save them, it was he. His abilities in public affairs had been proved; all Rome knew his character and attainments; he had now the further reputation of eminent saintliness. He was evidently the one man for the post; and accordingly he was unanimously elected by clergy, senate, and people. But he shrank from the proffered dignity. There was one way by which he might possibly escape it. No election of a pope could at this time take effect without the emperor's confirmation, and an embassy had to be sent to Constantinople to obtain it. Gregory therefore sent at the same time a letter to the emperor (Mauricius, who had succeeded Tiberius in 582), imploring him to withhold his confirmation; but it was intercepted by the prefect of the city, and another from the clergy, senate, and people sent in its place, entreating approval of their choice. During the interval that occurred, Gregory was active in his own way at Rome. He preached to the people, calling them to repentance; he also instituted what is known as the "Septiform Litany," to be chanted in procession through the streets of the city by seven companies of priests, of laymen, of monks, of virgins, of matrons, of widows, and of poor people and children, who, starting from different churches, were to meet for common supplication in the church of the Blessed Virgin. In it the words occur, peculiarly interesting to us as having been afterwards sung by his emissaries Augustin and his monks, as they marched into Canterbury at the commencement of their mission in this country: "We beseech thee, O Lord, in all thy mercy, that thy wrath and thine anger may be removed from this city, and from thy holy house. Allelujah." It was at the close of one of these processions that the incident is said to have occurred from which the Castle of St. Angelo has derived its name; the story being that Gregory saw on its site, above the monument of Hadrian, an angel sheathing his sword, as a token that the plague was stayed.

At length the imperial confirmation of his election arrived. He still refused; fled from the city in disguise, eluding the guards set to watch the gates, and hid himself in a forest cave. Pursued and discovered by means, it is said, of a supernatural light, he was brought back in triumph, conducted to the church of St. Peter, and at once ordained on the 3rd of September, 590. Flight to avoid the proffered dignity of the episcopate was not uncommon in those days, and might often be mere affectation, or compliance with the most approved custom. A law of the Emperor Leo (469), directed against canvassing for bishoprics, had even laid down as a rule, that no one ought to be ordained except greatly against his will; "he ought to be sought out, to be forced, when asked he should recede, when invited he should fly; for no one is worthy of the priesthood unless ordained against his will."[1] But there is no reason to doubt that Gregory felt a real reluctance, though he may have been partly actuated by the received view of what was proper in such a case, and though it may be suggested that he could hardly have thought seriously that flight from the city would in the end avail. Throughout his life he gives us the impression of a sincere man; he often afterwards recurs with regret to the peace of his convent; and it would be very unfair to him to question his sincerity, when he gives as his reason for refusal the fear lest "the worldly glory which he had cast away might creep on him under the colour of ecclesiastical government."

Five letters remain, written by him soon after his accession, in which he expresses his feelings on the occasion. They are addressed to John, patriarch of Constantinople, to Anastasius of Antioch, to Paulus Scholasticus in Sicily, to his closest friend Leander of Seville, and to Theoctista, the emperor's sister."[2] To the last, whose acquaintance he had doubtless made at Constantinople, and with whom, as being a pious lady of rank, it was according to his habit to

[1] *Lex Leonis, Cod. Justin.*, I. iii. 31.
[2] B. I., Ind. ix., epp. 3, 4, 5, 7, 43.

keep up correspondence, he wrote as follows:—
"Under the colour of the episcopate I have been brought back into the world; I am enslaved to greater earthly cares than I ever remember to have been subjected to as a layman. For I have lost the joys of my rest, and seem to have risen outwardly, while inwardly I have fallen. I lament that I am driven far away from my Maker's face. For I used to strive to live daily outside the world, outside the flesh; to drive from the eyes of the mind all phantasms of the body, and incorporeally to see supernal joys. . . . . Desiring nothing in this world, fearing nothing, I seemed to be standing on an eminence above the world, so that I almost thought the promise fulfilled in me, 'I will cause thee to ride upon the high places of the earth' (Is. lviii. 14). . . . . But suddenly driven from this eminence by the whirlwind of this temptation, I have fallen into fears and tremblings, since, though I fear nothing for myself, I am greatly afraid for those who have been committed to me. On all sides am I tossed by the waves of business, and pressed down by storms, so that I can say with truth, 'I am come into deep waters, where the floods overflow me' (Ps. lxix. 12) . . . . . I loved the beauty of the contemplative life, as a Rachel, barren, but beautiful and of clear vision, which, though on account of its quietness it is less productive, yet has a finer perception of the light. But, by what judgment I know not, Leah has been brought to me in the night, to wit the active life, fertile, but 'tender-eyed'; seeing less, though bringing forth more." . . . . He concludes, with a touch of humour, such as often enlivens even his most

serious letters, "Lo, my most serene lord the emperor has ordered an ape to be made a lion. And, indeed, in virtue of this order, a lion can the ape be called, but made one he cannot be. Wherefore my pious lord must needs lay the charge of all my faults and shortcomings not on me, but on himself, who has committed to one so weak an office of such excellence." His treatise also on "The Pastoral Care," written, as will appear in our review of his writings, with the immediate object of excusing his reluctance to accept the popedom,—shows evidently how a peculiarly deep sense of the responsibility of the episcopal office, and of risk to the souls of its bearers, had actuated him in his refusal.

Having been once placed in the high position he so little coveted, he rose to it at once, and fulfilled its multifarious duties with remarkable zeal and ability. His comprehensive policy, and his grasp of great issues, are not more remarkable than the minuteness of the details, in secular as well as religious matters, to which he was able to give his personal care. And this is the more striking in combination with the fact that, as many parts of his writings show, he remained all the time a monk at heart, thoroughly imbued with both the ascetic principles and the narrow credulity of contemporary monasticism. His private life, too, was still in a measure monastic: the monastic simplicity of his episcopal attire is noticed by his biographer; he lived with his clergy under strict rule, and in 595 issued a synodal decree substituting clergy for the boys and secular persons who had formerly waited on the pope in his chamber.

After sending, as was usual, a confession of his faith to the four Eastern patriarchs,—in which he declared his reception of the four Gospels, and of the four General Councils of Nice, Constantinople, Ephesus, and Chalcedon, speaking of the latter as the square stone on which the faith rests; and also his condemnation of the "three chapters" (above alluded to) which the Fifth Council called General had condemned,—one of his first measures was an attempt to induce the Bishops of Istria to assent to this condemnation. The Bishops of Italy generally had by this time assented, as the popes after Vigilius had also done: but those of Istria still held out. He therefore obtained an order from the emperor summoning them to Rome to attend a synod to be convened for the purpose, and wrote to Severus, the metropolitan of Aquileia, desiring him to attend with his suffragans. But they resisted his demand, affording an early instance during his reign of repudiation of papal claims. Having assembled in synods of their own, they petitioned the emperor to revoke his order, alleging that they only held what Pope Vigilius had taught them, objecting to the Bishop of Rome as their judge, on the ground of his being prejudiced in the matter of dispute, and undertaking to satisfy the emperor on the purity of their faith as soon as the state of Italy should permit their doing so. The emperor complied with their request, and wrote to Gregory commanding him, in consideration of the existing confusion of affairs, to give no further trouble to the Istrian bishops. And Gregory at once obeyed. Notwithstanding his undoubtedly high view of the authority of St. Peter's see, he always showed singular deference to the Imperial power. In his letter to Severus he had expressly mentioned "the command of the Most Christian and Most Serene Emperor" as supporting his summons; and writing afterwards to the Bishop of Ravenna, he says that he had refrained from further proceedings in obedience to "the commands of the most pious princes," adding that he would not cease to "write again to his most serene lords with the utmost zeal and freedom." Another instance of his attitude of obedience to the civil power in a matter on which he felt strongly may be mentioned here, though it occurred a few years later. The same Emperor Mauricius (A.D. 593) issued an edict, which he required the pope to publish in the West, forbidding soldiers to become monks during their period of service. This, though a reasonable requirement from the emperor's point of view, ran directly counter to the religious views of Gregory. Yet he at once published the edict, contenting himself with addressing pathetic remonstrances to the emperor, through the court physician Theodorus, in which he fully acknowledged the duty of submission. In his letter, which is characteristic of the writer both for its respectful tone and its plain speaking, as well as for its forcible language and the views maintained in it, he says: "He is guilty before Almighty God, who is not pure in all he does and says before our most serene lords. But in what I now suggest, I speak not as a bishop, nor as a public servant, but as a private person, because, most serene lord, you have been my lord from the time when you were not yet lord of the world. . . . . Which constitution (viz. the edict complained of) has filled me with great alarm, because by it the way to heaven is closed to many, and what has hitherto been lawful is made unlawful. For, though there are many who can combine a religious with a secular life, yet there are very many who can by no means be saved before God unless they leave all they have. But what am I, who speak this to my lords, but dust and a worm? Nevertheless, feeling that this law is against God the author of all things, I cannot be silent. For to this end has power over all men been given from heaven to my lords, that those who desire good things may be aided, that the way to heaven may be more widely opened, that the earthly may be subservient to the heavenly kingdom. And lo, it is now openly proclaimed that no one who has been once enlisted as an earthly soldier, unless dismissed for bodily weakness, or after completion of his service, shall be allowed to become a soldier of our Lord Jesus Christ. To this, by me, the last of His servants and yours, will Christ reply, 'From a notary I made thee a count of the body-guard; from a count of the body-guard I made thee a Cæsar; from a Cæsar I made thee an emperor; nay more, I have made thee also a father of emperors: I have committed my priests into thy hand; and dost thou withdraw thy soldiers from my service?' Answer thy servant, most pious lord, I pray thee, and say how thou wilt reply to thy Lord in the judgment, when He comes and thus speaks. . . . . And indeed it is a serious consideration that at this time especially any are forbidden to leave the world; a time when the very end of the world is at hand. For lo! there will be no delay: the heavens on fire, the earth on fire, the elements blazing, with angels and archangels, thrones and dominions, principalities and powers, the tremendous Judge will appear. Should He remit all other sins, and allege but this single law promulged against Himself, what excuse will there be? Wherefore by that tremendous Judge I implore thee, lest all the tears, all the prayers, all the alms of my lord should, on any ground, lose their lustre before the eyes of Almighty God. But let your piety, either by interpretation or alteration, modify the force of this law; since the army of my lords against their enemies is the more replenished when the army of God is replenished for prayer." He concludes, "And now, I have on both sides discharged my duty. On the one I have yielded obedience to the emperor; on the other I have not been silent in the cause of God."[1]

It is to be observed that in this remonstrance he showed discrimination and willingness to concede what he could. He allowed the reasonableness of forbidding soldiers to take holy orders, because in this case they might only be wishing to change one form of worldliness for another. But he argues that no such worldly motives could operate in drawing them to the monastic life, and that to impede them in their aspirations was to fight against God. And he appeals to numbers of cases, known to himself, in which soldiers who had become monks had been saintly converts, and had even worked miracles.

[1] B. III., Ind. xi., ep. 65.

It would seem, however, that further experience led him to see the necessity of placing some restriction on the liberty for which he had so earnestly pleaded, for in 598 he addressed a circular to various metropolitans and other bishops, accompanied by the Imperial law above referred to, in which, while he decidedly discountenances the hasty ordination of any who had been engaged in secular offices, whether civil or military, he directs that they are not even to be received into monasteries till released from their worldly obligations, not till after strict inquiry into their lives, and a probation of three years before assuming the monastic habit. He adds, "In which matter, believe me, the most serene and most Christian emperor is entirely satisfied, and willingly allows the conversion of those whom he knows not to be implicated in public duties."[1] The emperor may be concluded from these expressions to have yielded so far to Gregory's remonstrances as to use moderation in the enforcement of the law, and to have come to an amicable understanding with him on this subject.

In his second year (591) his orthodox zeal was directed against another form of heresy, that of the Donatists in Africa. It has been said already that the African Church, having been delivered through the reconquest of Africa under Justinian (533) from about a century of persecution under the Arian Vandals, had since that time submitted willingly to the authority of the Roman see, though in an earlier age (notably under St. Cyprian in the 3rd century) it had asserted consider-

[1] B. VIII., Ind. i., ep. 5.

able independence. But the old Donatist sect,[1] which had originated there as early as 311, in spite of severe measures of repression in past times, lingered there still, and seems at this time not only to have been spreading itself, but also maintaining friendly relations with the orthodox, and tolerated by their bishops, some of whom were accused of ordaining Donatists under the influence of bribes. It was the custom in Numidia for the senior bishop, whatever his see, to assume the primacy, and so interfused were the two parties in that province that a Donatist primate had thus come to exercise jurisdiction over the Catholic bishops. Such a system of comprehension, and, indeed, Donatism altogether, Gregory, ever intolerant of all forms of heresy or schism, set himself resolutely to oppose. He kept up a correspondence, lasting through several years, with the African bishops, and especially with Dominicus, bishop of Carthage, and Columbus of Numidia, urging them to hold synods for the correction of such abuses and for the suppression of Donatism. The latter prelate, whose devotion to the

[1] The sect of the Donatists had originated in North Africa at the beginning of the fourth century, being a secession from the Church on the ground of the then Bishop of Carthage (Cæcilian) having been ordained by another bishop (Felix of Aptunga) who was accused of being a "traditor," *i.e.*, one who had given up the Holy Scriptures of his church to the civil authorities during the Diocletian persecution. This unfaithfulness was held by the seceders to have incapacitated him from transmitting the apostolical succession. Hence they set up a rival bishop to Cæcilian; first Majorinus, and then Donatus, surnamed "the Great," who transmitted the Donatist succession. They were not, strictly speaking, heretics, though schismatics, regarding themselves as the only true Church.

see of Rome is praised highly by his correspondent, seems to have incurred the enmity of many of his colleagues on account of it: an evidence, by the way, that the claims of Rome were not even yet fully acknowledged in Africa. To this enmity Gregory alludes in one of his letters, and encourages Columbus by reminding him that the good must ever be exposed to the hatred of the wicked. He had recourse also to the civil arm, writing urgently, at the outset of his proceedings, to Gennadius, the exarch of Africa, desiring him to admonish the Catholic bishops how to proceed in the matter, and exhorting him to fight as valiantly against the enemies of the Church as he had done against those of the State, to repress the attempts of heretics, and subdue their proud necks to the yoke of rectitude. He continued to write to him with the same purport, and in 596 complained to the Emperor himself of the Imperial laws against the African Donatists not being adequately enforced.[1]

His conduct in this case suggests the question how far Gregory approved of persecution as a means of suppressing error. When we consider how recently in the history of the Church any theories of tolerance have prevailed, we cannot with reason expect to find him maintaining them. Accordingly he did afterwards encourage the Catholic rulers of the Franks to use force in their dominions; in the papal possessions in Sicily he ordered the Manicheans to be recalled to the faith by vigorous persecution, and elsewhere the peasants on his estates to be recovered from heathenism, if freemen, by exactions and imprisonment, and,

[1] B. I., Ind. ix., ep. 61; B. IV., Ind. xii., ep. 7; B. VI., Ind. xiv., ep. 63; B. VI., Ind. xiv., ep. 65.

if slaves, by "blows and torments." But, on the other hand, he showed a spirit of unusual forbearance towards Jews. In the same letter which orders the severe persecution of Manicheans, he directs Jews to be attracted to the faith, rather than compelled, by the remission of one-third of the taxes due to the Church in the case of such as might conform; and even for this appeal to interested motives he makes a sort of apology, saying that, though the conversions thus obtained might be insincere, yet the children of the converts would be baptized as Christians. Further, we find letters to three bishops, one of whom had driven Jews from their synagogue, and the others had converted many by offering them the option of conformity or exile, in which letters he strongly condemns such measures. "Conversions," says he, "wrought by force are never sincere, and such as are so converted seldom fail to return to their vomit as soon as the force is removed." Again, "Those who differ from the Christian religion should be gathered to the unity of the faith by gentleness, kindness, admonition, persuasion, lest those whom the sweetness of preaching and the fear of future judgment might have invited to believe, be repelled by threats and terrors." Here we have sentiments expressed which many in ages boasting of superior enlightenment might often have studied with advantage. And if his action in some cases seems to discredit these professions, it is but an instance of human inconsistency. The humanity and good sense thus expressed is no less real, though warped sometimes by the impulses of zeal in accordance with current views.

CHAPTER III.

Correction of Monastic Abuses—Separation of Monks and Clergy—Exemption of Monasteries from Episcopal Control—Case of Venantius—Nunneries—Sanctity of Marriage—Endowments—Election of Bishops—Confirmation—Use of the Pall—Respect for Episcopal Rights—Januarius of Cagliari—Natalis of Salona—Correction of Clerks—Sanctuary—Privileges of Clergy—Celibacy—Administration of the Patrimony—Charities.

BEFORE proceeding further to note in order the leading events of Gregory's episcopate, let us take a general view of the manner of his administration, especially with regard to discipline, selecting in illustration a few salient instances.

He was no less diligent from the beginning of his reign in correcting abuses among the orthodox monks and clergy, in Italy and elsewhere, than in his attempts to suppress heresy. It is to be observed that at that time the distinction was marked between the monastic and clerical orders. The exercise of clerical functions was accounted inconsistent with the seclusion of monastic life. Gregory himself had indeed, though a monk, been ordained deacon by Pope Benedict in order to qualify him for his mission to Constantinople, and as a deacon he returned to his monastery. But monks, as such, were laymen.

The whole theory of the monastic life as conceived by Gregory was that those devoted to it should be secluded from the world with all its affairs and temptations, should live altogether in the spiritual sphere, engaged in reading, prayer, and heavenly contemplation; thus alone could the closest communication with Heaven be attained, and the way of salvation secured from risk; and with such a life holy orders were considered as inconsistent as purely secular occupations were, for they were understood then as necessarily involving pastoral responsibility, and intercourse with the world. A priest might, indeed, become a monk, as was the case with the great father of monasticism in the West, St. Jerome; but in this case he must cease to officiate as a priest, even within his convent, for priestly responsibility was one thing, the monastic life another. Gregory showed the importance he attached to this theory by ordering, after his accession, that no monk after ordination should be allowed to remain in his monastery, and no priest to enter one except to perform necessary priestly offices, or become a monk without relinquishing clerical ministrations. He also promoted the system, which proved in after-ages of such practical importance, of exempting monasteries from episcopal superintendence, to which they had originally been always subject, and which had been insisted on by a canon of the Council of Chalcedon. In many cases indeed he directed bishops to correct the irregularities of monks according to the old system, but in others forbade them to celebrate mass in person within the walls of convents, to ordain their inmates without the abbat's leave, to interfere with their revenues or require an account of them, or to burden them by demanding entertainment. In particular instances he exempted convents from all episcopal interference, except for ordaining abbats chosen by the monks, or commissioning priests to say mass when required. He seems to have become more adverse to the old system as his experience grew; for lastly, in the Lateran Council held under him, A.D. 601, he issued a general decree to all bishops, confirming the liberties of monasteries everywhere, and exempting them in all respects from episcopal control. He also was active in correcting the prevailing irregularities of monks, which Benedict's reform had failed to extirpate. A great number of his letters, addressed to various persons in various places, are on this subject. In some cases he animadverts on the wandering habits of monks, or their relapse to secular life, or even to the enormity of marriage;[1] in others, on the evils arising in convents from the laxity or the undue severity of abbats. To one abbat he writes, "As the careless remissness of thy deceased predecessor saddened us, so thy solicitude rejoices us. Restrain therefore those who are committed to thee from gluttony, pride, avarice, vain discourse, and all uncleanness. In which correction know that this order is to be observed, that thou love the persons but persecute their vices, lest, shouldest thou act otherwise, correction pass into cruelty, and thou ruin those whom thou desirest to amend."[2]

As an instance of laxity of discipline, a case occurs where the monks were in the habit of leaving their convent and wandering where they pleased whenever their abbat attempted to enforce the rule.[3] Of one way in which severe discipline might be exercised we

[1] B. I., Ind. ix., epp. 41, 42, &c.
[2] B. XI., Ind. iv., ep. 12.
[3] B. VII., Ind. xv., ep. 35.

find a curious instance in St. Gregory's Dialogues, where he tells us of a saintly monk called Libertinus, whom his superior in a fit of anger, not having a rod at hand, beat over the head and face with a footstool till he was black and blue. In this case the discipline had no bad moral effect on the sufferer, but the contrary; for with exemplary patience he submitted without complaint, and being afterwards asked how his face had come into so sad a plight, showed his regard at once to his superior and to truth by replying, "Yesterday, for my sins, I came in contact with a footstool, and suffered this."[1]

Among the letters in connection with monasticism are some to Venantius, a noble Roman, who had given up monastic life and married. He pleads with him in most urgent strains to return, reminding him, among other things, that if Ananias was struck dead for abstracting money due to God, much sorer judgment must be due to one who has abstracted himself. He failed, however, in his attempt to reclaim him, and was unable, or unwilling, in this case to insist on the rule in other cases laid down of requiring such renegades to return under pain of excommunication, for he afterwards carried on a friendly correspondence with him, sent compliments to his daughters, and sympathized with him under an attack of gout. In one of his letters he refers to a serious quarrel between Venantius and his bishop, in the course of which the armed retainers of the former had made an attack on one Episcopius, and the bishop had repelled him from communion. Gregory on this occasion wrote

[1] Greg. Dial. B. I., ch. 2.

in a very courteous and conciliatory tone to his noble friend, whom, from personal regard, or desire of keeping up influence over him, or from both motives combined, he seems anxious not to offend, excusing the conduct of the bishop, and exhorting to reconciliation. He also desired the bishop, in a letter addressed to him, to condone the offence of Venantius, and to allow masses to be celebrated in his house, as had been done before the quarrel, and even to officiate in person if desired. But, while he thus bore with the noble renegade, he never gave up the hope of reclaiming him at last to the fulfilment of his early vows, for, on hearing of his dangerous illness in the year 601, he wrote to John, bishop of Syracuse, desiring him to press the subject on the dying man :— " The first care which your holiness must not neglect is to bid him think of his soul, exhorting him, imploring him, putting before him the terrible judgment of God, and promising him His unspeakable mercy, that he may return, even at the last hour, to the monastic life, lest the guilt of so great a fault stand against him in the eternal judgment." In the same letter, with characteristic tenderness, he shows equal solicitude for the two daughters of his friend, Barbara and Antonina, now about to be left orphans, whom as being likely from some cause to be involved in difficulties, the father had commended to the Pope's protection. To them, also, his "most sweet daughters," he wrote a tender, fatherly letter, which is worth quoting at length :—" Having received your letter, which speaks in tears rather than in words, I am affected no less than you, most beloved daughters, by grief for your father's illness, for we cannot regard as extraneous the sadness which has been made our own by the law of charity. But, since in no despair is the compassion of our Redeemer to be distrusted, cheer up your spirits for your father's comfort, and place all your hope in the hand of Almighty God. And we trust in His protection that He will guard you from all adversity, and cheer your tribulation, and mercifully grant your affairs to be arranged according to your father's desires. But should he pay the debt of humanity, let not any despair overwhelm you, nor the words of any person terrify you, for, after God, who is the governor and protector of orphans, we will be so solicitous for your necessities, and, with God's help, to hasten to provide as we can for your interests, that no attempts of unjust men may disturb you, that we may repay in all things the debt we owe to the goodness of your parents. So may heavenly grace nourish you with its favour, defend you by its protection from all evils, so that the happiness of your life may be our joy."[1] The above account of Gregory's correspondence with and about Venantius has involved some digression from the subject immediately before us, viz. his measures with respect to monks and monasteries, but it seemed too interesting to be passed by, bringing out as it does the considerateness and tenderness of the man, never quenched by ascetic theories. Considering his severe view of the sinfulness of the marriage of Venantius, there is something peculiarly graceful in his passing allusion to their deceased mother in his letter to the sorrowing

---

[1] B. I., Ind. ix., ep. 34; B. VI., Ind. xiv., ep. 43; B. IX., Ind. ii., ep. 123; B. XI., Ind. iv., epp. 30, 35, 36.

daughter, when he speaks of the goodness to himself of both their parents.

Nunneries also, which were not always what they should have been, received an equal share of his attention. In some cases nuns had left their convent, and even married: such he orders to be sent back to seclusion and penance, and all who should obstruct their return to be excommunicated.[1] We find allusions to scandals, in one instance from a medical man having been allowed access to a nunnery.[2] Some bishops are reproved for not looking better after the state of the female communities under their jurisdiction;[3] in other cases he protects such communities from interference with their rights or endowments.

There is, however, no sufficient reason from his letters to conclude that abuses of the kind complained of were the general rule in convents, though there was evidently a liability to them, and they not unfrequently occurred. In one of his letters he objects strongly to a scheme that was afoot of founding a monastery of men in the neighbourhood of a female one, which shows his sense of the inconveniences that might attend such an arrangement.[4] The following are among the regulations he made for the rectifying of abuses, some of which show what good sense modified his monastic zeal. No man was to become a monk under eighteen years of age; two years of probation

---

[1] B. IV., Ind. xii., epp. 9, 27; B. VIII., Ind. i., epp. 8, 9.
[2] B. V., Ind. xiii., ep. 6. [3] B. IV., Ind. xii., ep. 9.
[4] B. XI., Ind. iv., ep. 25.

were always to be required (Benedict's rule having required only one year), and, in the case of soldiers, three years; no married person was to be received unless both the man and wife were willing to embrace the monastic life. He spoke strongly on this last point, showing how clearly, notwithstanding his monastic predilections, he recognised the sanctity of marriage. "For," he writes on one occasion, "when two have been made one flesh by the bond of marriage, it is incongruous that one part should be converted, and the other part remain in the world." Again, "If any say that marriages ought to be dissolved for the sake of religion, let them know that, though human law has allowed this, yet divine law has forbidden it. For the Truth Himself says, 'Those whom God hath joined together, let not man put asunder.' Who then may contradict this heavenly legislator? For we know how it is written, 'They two shall be one flesh.'" In one instance he ordered a husband who had gone into a monastery without his wife's consent to be immediately sent back to her, even though he should have received the tonsure.[1] He further laid down the rule that not even an abbat was to leave his convent except on urgent occasions, and no one ever alone; that no monk or nun should retain any private possession; that no young woman was to be made an abbess, and none "veiled" (*i.e.* finally and irrevocably consecrated by solemn ceremony to virginity) under sixty years of age. Forty appears to have been the previous limit of age fixed by canons of councils.[2]

[1] B. VI., Ind. xiv., ep. 48; B. XI., Ind. iv., epp 45, 50.
[2] *See* Bingham, B. VII., ch. iv. sect. 6.

Further, in order to secure to the monastic communities the freedom from worldly cares which the theory of their life required, he was careful to provide them with endowments, and to protect them in the possession of such as had been assigned to them by bequests or otherwise. He contributed largely from the revenues of "the patrimony" for this purpose, in some cases causing monasteries to be rebuilt and refounded; and in Corsica, where before his time there had been none, founding new ones. He evinced his accustomed attention to details in reference to such matters, laying down accurately the amount and sources of revenue to be enjoyed by various communities: assigning, for instance, to a nunnery in one case, as a condition of the bishop being allowed to consecrate it, a revenue of ten solidi free of taxes, together with three male servants, three yoke of oxen, five slaves, ten mares, ten cows, a prescribed number of vines, forty sheep &c., "according to custom."

The state of the clergy called for and received equal attention with that of the monastic orders. In the exercise of his patriarchal jurisdiction we find him rebuking and sometimes deposing bishops, writing them letters of direction and advice, appointing commissions to inquire into charges against them, and to take action during the vacancy of sees. On the death of a bishop, the visitor appointed by him for the purpose was to see to the canonical election of a successor by clergy and people, and to his fitness for the office. Fitness consisted in such points as

[1] B. XI., Ind. iv., ep. 66.

these:—he must be already in Holy Orders, not bound to any secular office, free from bodily defects, of good life and conversation, well-versed in Holy Scripture, and especially the Psalms, benevolent and charitable; not a youth, or one who had married a second wife or a widow, or who had young children. He was to be chosen from among the clergy of the church he was to rule, if a proper candidate could be found among them, but not otherwise. Above all things simony in all forms was to be strictly forbidden, nor were powerful persons to be allowed to influence elections. The election having been made, Gregory still reserved to himself the right of granting or withholding confirmation, and there were many cases in which he withheld it. For example, in 591 he directs Severus, whom he had appointed visitor of the Church of Ariminum during a vacancy, to disallow an election that had been made, without giving any definite reason, and to require the inhabitants either to select a more fit candidate, or to appoint the person indicated by himself. In 595, two persons having been chosen for the bishopric of Naples by two parties in the church there, he rejects both; one because he had a young daughter, the other because he was too "simple" for the post, and because he was reported to have given his money on usury. He directs, however, the charges against the second candidate to be more fully inquired into, but requires the Neapolitans to nominate a third person for consecration, in the event of these charges being established.[1]

[1] B. I., Ind. ix., ep. 57; B. X., Ind. iii., ep. 62; cf. B. V., Ind. xiii., ep. 48; B. IV., Ind. xii., ep. 20.

In some cases, when the Lombard invasion had caused episcopal cities to be insecure or depopulated, he authorized the transference or amalgamation of sees.[1] With one metropolitan, John of Ravenna, he had a long dispute about the use of the pallium. This article of ecclesiastical costume, sent by the popes to metropolitans by way of connecting them and their jurisdiction with the see of Rome, was worn by them ordinarily in the celebration of Mass only. John wore it on other occasions, pleading the ancient custom of the Church of Ravenna. Gregory denied any authorization from Rome of this custom, which he regarded as savouring of pride, and forbade its continuance. John, however, though writing to the pope with the utmost respect, persisted till his death. His successor, Marinianus (who had been a monk with Gregory at St. Andrew's in Rome) continued the contest, which was at length compromised by his being allowed to wear the pallium as formerly on four great festivals during the year.[2] In Sicily, where great laxity seems to have prevailed, there had been no metropolitan, the bishops having been directly subject to the bishop of Rome. There at first a general supervision of the Church was committed to the subdeacon Peter, who had been sent as "ruler of the patrimony"; and afterwards Maximinianus, bishop of Syracuse (Gregory's predecessor in the abbacy of St. Andrew's), was made the Pope's vicar for ecclesiastical purposes, and had the pallium sent him, but on the understanding that

[1] B. I., epp. 78, 80; B. II., Ind. x., ep. 37.
[2] B. III., Ind. xi., ep. 57; B. V., Ind. xiii., epp. 11, 15, 56.

the vicariate should not be considered as permanently attached to his see. In 596 John, who succeeded Maximinianus, had the same jurisdiction, with the pallium, assigned to him.[1] The Sicilian bishops, who were nine in number, had been required by Pope Leo to visit the threshold of the Apostles, each once in three years. Gregory, in the interest, we may suppose, of their dioceses, substituted five years for three. But, while he thus claimed and exercised such large powers of supervision and discipline over bishops and metropolitans, he was careful to respect and defend their traditional rights, to allow them ordinarily free action when once appointed, and never unnecessarily to interfere with their canonical election. Writing in 592 to Dominicus of Carthage, in Africa, where (as has been seen) some jealousy of his interference was felt, he thus expresses his principles in this regard:— "But as to what your fraternity has written about ecclesiastical privileges, have no doubt whatever about this, that, as we defend our own rights, so we preserve those of every single Church. I neither grant to any one, through favour, more than he has a claim to, nor, through ambition, derogate from the just rights of any: but I desire to honour my brethren in all respects, but that each should be so honoured that his rights be not opposed to those of another."[2] It would be highly unjust to accuse Pope Gregory of a policy of aggression in his ecclesiastical government. Whether or not the large powers he claimed were in

[1] B. II., Ind. x., ep. 23; B. VI., Ind. xiv., ep. 18.
[2] B. II., Ind. x., ep. 47.

accordance with the primitive constitution of the Church is not the question before us. All we say is that they were such as he sincerely believed to belong to St. Peter's see, and such as popes had claimed before him, though none had brought them to bear with equal power and system. And it cannot be doubted that he used them so as to benefit the Church at large. Nor is his tone ever harsh or domineering. One old bishop (Januarius of Cagliari, in Sardinia) he spares on account of his grey hairs, though he seems to have been a very unsatisfactory character. There are many letters to him or about him. He was culpably remiss in looking after the female convents; he charged exorbitant burial fees; on one occasion he had on Sunday before mass reaped a neighbour's crop, and after officiating had returned to remove his landmark. For this last offence Gregory writes to him, "Since we still spare thy grey hairs, we exhort thee, wretched old man, to bethink thee in time, and restrain thyself from such levity of manners and perversity of deeds. Sentence might have been launched against thee; but, knowing thy simplicity together with thy age, we are in the meantime silent. Those under whose counsel thou hast done these things we excommunicate for two months, but so that if they should die within this time they be not refused the viaticum. But guard against their counsels for the future, lest, if thou be their pupil in evil whose master thou oughtest to be in good, we spare henceforth neither thy simplicity nor thy old age."[1]

[1] B. IX., Ind. ii., ep. 1.

Another bishop (Natalis of Salona), whom he had reprehended for addiction to banquets, and who had defended his practice by Scripture arguments, he answers in a good-humoured strain. To the bishop's adducing of the example of Abraham entertaining the three angels, Gregory replies, "Not even we would blame your blessedness in respect of feasts if we were aware that you were in the habit of entertaining angels as guests"; and in another part of his letter says, "Your holiness rightly praises banquets in common which are made with the intention of charity; but these only proceed from charity in which no absent person is backbitten, no one derided, no idle stories about secular affairs, but the words of sacred reading are heard; where no more is taken than is necessary for refreshing the weakness of the body that it may be kept in health for the practice of virtue. If your banquets are of this sort, I confess that you are masters of abstainers."[1]

He gave frequent and detailed directions also with respect to the inferior clergy, holding that "bad priests are the cause of the people's ruin," that "what is but a fault in laymen is a crime in clergymen," and "that a clergy corrupt within cannot long stand in relation to the world outside." We find continual admonitions to legates, metropolitans, and others, that they should inquire into and correct reported clerical delinquencies by excommunication, degradation, imprisonment, and even in one case by stripes. He forbade any to be ordained who were engaged in any public office, civil or military: he recalled itinerant

[1] B. II., Ind. x., ep. 52.

clerks to their sphere of work, and most urgently he pressed upon all the paramount duty of succouring the poor and oppressed. With this view he maintained the right of asylum in churches and their precincts, but not so as thereby to defeat the ends of justice. Maurilio, for instance, an ex-prefect of Ravenna, having fled into sanctuary from the prosecution of the prefect Georgius, he directed the bishop to protect him there, but is careful to add, "not that we doubt (far from it!) the justice of the most excellent Lord Prefect Georgius, one whose proved character in the administration of his dignified office we are well assured of, but that the glorious Maurilio may on his side defend his cause without suspicion of oppression."[1] Again, to Romanus, his defensor in Sicily, he writes, "We have been informed that certain men of small discretion desire to implicate us in their own perils, and to be so defended by ecclesiastical persons that the latter may be themselves held parties to their misdeeds. Wherefore, I hereby admonish thee, and through thee our brother and fellow-bishop John, and others whom it may concern, so to regulate your ecclesiastical protection that no one implicated in public theft may appear to be unjustly defended by us, lest, by attempting indiscreet defence, we transfer to ourselves the reputation of evil-doers. But, as far as becomes the Church, by admonitions and intercessions, succour those whom you can, so as both to afford them help, and to avoid injury to the reputation of the Church."[2] A

[1] B. I., Ind. ix., ep. 37.
[2] B. IX., Ind. ii., ep. 27.

reference to lay tribunals was forbidden to the clergy, who were regarded as an order apart, and amenable only to their ecclesiastical superiors. Further, their claim to exemption from the civil jurisdiction, even in criminal cases, and at the suit of laymen, which caused such conflict between Church and State in a later age, had its support in the position taken by Gregory on the subject. He writes to Bonifacius, his defensor in Corsica, " If any one has a cause against a clerk, let him refer it to his bishop. Should the bishop be suspected, let him (*i.e.* the bishop), or, should this be objected to by the prosecutor, do you yourself depute some one who shall compel the parties to choose arbitrators by mutual consent; by whom whatever shall be decided, whether through thy solicitude or the bishop's, let it be carried out in all respects, that there may be no case for further litigation."[1]

In all the clergy he required strict celibacy; they were to have no women in their houses but mothers, sisters, or wives married before ordination, from whom they were to live separately.[2] Bishops he recommends to imitate Augustine by banishing from their houses even such female relatives as the canons allowed.[3]

But even in matters of this kind, however important he considered them, he could show forbearance and discretion. In Sicily the rule of celibacy had, in 588, been extended to sub-deacons. This rule he

[1] B. XI., Ind. iv., ep. 77.
[2] B. I., Ind. ix., ep. 52; B. XI., Ind. iv., ep. 69.
[3] B. IX., Ind. ii., ep. 60; B. XIII., Ind. vi., epp. 35, 36.

enforced so far as to order bishops to require a vow of celibacy from all future sub-deacons; but, owning the hardship of the rule on those who had made no promise at their ordination, he contented himself with forbidding advancement to the diaconate of existing sub-deacons who had lived with wives.[1] Simony also, which appears to have been very prevalent, he did all he could to suppress, and set the example by himself refusing the annual presents which the bishops of Rome had received from their suffragans, or payment for palls sent to metropolitans. Payments under the last head were forbidden in perpetuity by a Roman synod held under him in 595.

Secular matters also in connection with the administration of the papal estates received from him careful and minute attention. Indeed the extent, evinced by the voluminous collection of his letters, to which he was able to make himself acquainted with, and direct the details of, business of all kinds both sacred and secular, in so many regions of the world, is remarkable. The see of Rome had large possessions, constituting what was called the "Patrimony of St. Peter," not only in Italy and the adjoining islands, but also in remoter parts, including Illyria, Gaul, Dalmatia, and even Africa and the East. They were managed by officers called "Rulers of the Patrimony," and "Defensores," to whom Gregory continually wrote, directing them about the management of the farms and the protection of the peasants. He was very particular on the latter head. Their

[1] B. I., Ind. ix., ep. 44.

payments were fixed, and they were to be allowed to make them by instalments, assisted by loans; dues payable on the marriages of serfs were lowered, and legal forms of security were to be furnished to peasants, so as to provide against the recurrence of oppression; the families of farmers were secured in their succession to tenancy, and their rights in other ways guarded. He enters into very minute particulars on such matters, taking anxious care lest the claims of the Church should be pressed so as to trench on private rights, or cause hardship or wrong to any.[1] It may be here observed that the possession by the Pope of this extensive patrimony, and Gregory's careful supervision of it, had an important result as securing the temporal independence of the Roman See. He did not indeed by any means set up on the strength of it a claim to independent sovereignty. He ever professed himself, and acted as, a loyal subject of the Emperor. But, including as it did several important cities, Nepte in Tuscany, Otranto, Gallipoli, and, as some assert, Naples, and as the political state of affairs at the time allowed, and even necessitated, the Pope's unfettered sway over it, it undoubtedly gave him a sort of princely position which he could not otherwise have maintained, and paved the way to the independent sovereignty of a later age.

The revenues accruing from the Patrimony were expended under Gregory's personal superintendence according to the fourfold division customary in the West—to the bishop, to the clergy, to the

---

[1] B. I., Ind. ix., ep. 42.

fabrics and services of the Church, and to the poor. He was unbounded in his charitable donations; a great part of the population of Rome depended on them; daily when he sat down to dinner a portion was sent to the poor at his door; he had the poor and infirm searched out in every street, and kept a large book for the names of the objects of his bounty.

Such prodigal almsgiving might of course, for aught we know, encourage and perpetuate indolence and pauperism. But it would be absurd to look for modern principles of political economy in St. Gregory. Those saints of old time interpreted literally the Gospel precepts about almsgiving, and at any rate they did not evade them. And, indeed, the state of Rome at that time appears to have been such as left no alternatives but general almsgiving or starvation. The population, long accustomed, even in prosperous times, to depend on the doles of the rich, was now, thinned though it was by plague and famine, out of proportion to the ordinary supply of food; fields of industry were cut off, the country round was devastated, and never safe from the Lombards. Whether or not there was truth in the cries of the populace after his death, blaming his too prodigal expenditure for the famine which then ensued, there was undoubtedly during his reign an abnormal need of succour; and among the Christian virtues of Gregory we are justified in estimating highly his personal self-denial and his unbounded charity to the poor.

CHAPTER IV.

The Church in Spain—Letters to Leander and Reccared—Appeal of two Spanish Bishops to Rome—Correspondence with Irish Bishops—St. Columban's letters—Eastern Illyricum—Hadrianus—Natalis—Maximus—Remonstrance with the Emperor—Letter to the Empress—Final settlement—Claim to authority over the Eastern Church—Letter to John the Faster—Lombard Invasion—Gregory's Sermons—Patriotic activity—Thwarted by the Exarch—Letters to the Emperor and Empress—Truce with the Lombards—John the Faster calls himself Universal Bishop—Gregory's view of the question—His remonstrances—His sarcastic vein—He addresses the Patriarchs of Antioch and Alexandria—Cyriacus succeeds John the Faster—Gregory's renewed remonstrance—Correspondence with the Patriarchs—His view of St. Peter's Primacy being shared by Antioch and Alexandria—Renewed Lombard invasions—Gregory's activity—Results of his efforts (591-596).

HAVING now seen something generally of Gregory's work and character during his career as pope, we may resume the thread of his history, noticing in order its principal events, and dwelling on those of most interest and importance.

It has been already mentioned that in 589, the year before his accession, Reccared, the Visigothic king of Spain, had, at the Council of Toledo, renounced Arianism for Catholicity. In this important event Gregory naturally felt a warm interest. He was informed of it by Leander, Archbishop of Seville, whose acquaintance he had made at Constantinople; and to him he wrote letters on the occasion glowing with thankfulness, sympathy, and affection; sending him on one occasion part of his commentary on the book of Job, which had been begun (as has been seen) in concert with him at Constantinople; on another, a pall, to be worn at mass only, with the benediction of St. Peter. These letters to one who appears to have been his dearest and most confidential friend are remarkable for the deep sense expressed of the misery of the burdens of office, especially in the lamentable state of things then existing, and his regret for past monastic peace. He speaks with humility of his own character having suffered from the change, and disclaims the compliments which his correspondent had addressed to him. "I am not now, good man," he says, "he whom you used to know. I have advanced outwardly, I confess; but inwardly I have fallen. . . . Much does this burdensome honour oppress me; innumerable cares din through me, and, when my mind collects itself for God, they cleave me as if with swords. My heart has no rest: it lies prostrated in the lowest depths by the weight of its own cogitation: seldom or never does the wing of contemplation raise it aloft. . . . But, fallen as I am into these waves of perturbation, I beseech thee by Almighty God to hold me up by the hand of thy prayer. I sailed as it were with a favouring breeze, when I led a tranquil life in the monastery; but suddenly a stormy tempest rose and carried me away, and I lost my prosperous course. Now am I tost with waves, and seek the plank of thy intercession, that, though not accounted worthy to come rich, with my ship entire, to shore, I may at any rate reach it on a plank after loss." In one of his letters to Leander he gives proof of more liberality of view with respect to forms than was often displayed by popes. Three immersions in baptism were the Roman usage, which he calls in his letter "sacraments" of the three days of Christ's burial; or, he adds, they may be taken by some to denote the three Persons of the Undivided Trinity. But, inasmuch as this had been the usage of the Arians in Spain, and regarded by them as expressing their heretical docrine on the Trinity, he fully agrees with Leander in approving single immersion in the Spanish Church, notwithstanding the different use of the Church of Rome. "For," says he, "when there is one faith, difference of usage does no harm to the Church." He wrote also to Reccared, the royal convert, exhorting him to humility, chastity, and mercy; thanking him for presents received, and sending him in return a key from the body of St. Peter, containing iron from the chain that had bound him, a cross containing a portion of the true one, and some hairs of John the Baptist. Such presents were well adapted for exciting the superstitious reverence of the king, and there is no reason to suppose, from what we know of Gregory, that he himself doubted the genuineness or the efficacy of the relics. The pall sent to Leander is the only known instance of this emblem of metropolitan jurisdiction having been in early days received from Rome by the Catholic Church of Spain, which was not for long afterwards, notwithstanding Gregory's early patronage, marked for its dependence on the popes.

We find, however, Gregory after this (apparently in 603, towards the end of his life) taking action in the case of two bishops, Januarius and Stephanus, alleged to have been unjustly and uncanonically deposed in Spain through the action of a powerful noble. He commissioned one John, whom he sent as *Defensor Ecclesiæ* into the country, to examine and adjudicate on the cases, and furnished him with extracts from imperial laws providing for the immunity of clergy from secular judgments, and for reference of their causes to metropolitans and patriarchs, or, in the absence of patriarchs, finally to the Apostolic See, as being "the head of all churches." John's adjudication on the cases is also extant, in which he decided in favour of the deposed bishops. Whether or not this decision, arising probably from an appeal of the aggrieved prelates, was accepted and carried out by the authorities in Spain, there is no evidence to show. There is no reason for concluding that it was not. At any rate it illustrates the Pope's own view of the authority of his see.

In 592 we find him in correspondence with the bishops of Ireland, who, like those of Istria, still refused to join in the condemnation of the "three chapters," and, like them, stood out against the Pope on the subject. They had, it appears, sent him a letter, no longer extant, in which they had spoken of some persecution from which their church was suffering, had defended their position with respect to the "chapters," and attributed the Lombard invasion to divine judgment on the Pope for his acquiescence in their condemnation. He replies that they must by no means glory in their persecution, or expect the rewards of martyrdom, as long as they kept aloof from Catholic unity in the matter of the "three chapters"; he defends submission to the fifth Council, which had condemned these chapters, on the ground that the condemnation did not touch the faith as previously defined, but only affected three persons, one of whom at least had evidently written what was heretical, and was therefore "not unjustly condemned." This way of putting the case seems to imply some doubt in Gregory's own mind as to the whole of the position which he had to defend. He seems to have felt a difficulty himself as to the condemnation of the two writers at least who had been acquitted of heresy by the Council of Chalcedon. But he sends the Irish bishops the treatise on the subject which his predecessor, Pelagius, had written, which he tells them must convince them, unless they were more obstinate than reasonable. As to the Lombard invasion, it is, he says, no proof of divine judgment on himself, but rather of fatherly correction. The Irish were not probably thus convinced, though Baronius in his history takes it for granted that they were. For there is a letter extant from the noted Irish Saint Columban to Pope Boniface IV., written in 614, in which the latter is freely blamed, in a tone of irony, for continuing to condemn the "three chapters." The following remarkable words occur in it: "Watch, I pray thee, pope, watch; and again I say, watch. For perhaps Vigilius did not watch well, whom those who

throw blame on you call the author of this scandal."
(Here is a sly allusion to the tergiversation of Pope
Vigilius.) "From the time when the Son of God, in
those two fervent horses of the Holy Ghost, rode
through the sea of the nations, &c. . . . the supreme
charioteer of that chariot, who is Christ, came Himself even to us." He means that the Irish, having
received the Gospel, had at any rate Christ for their
founder, though they could not boast of St. Peter and
St. Paul, like Rome. "From that time you have been
great and illustrious, and Rome herself has become
more great and distinguished than before; and you,
if we may so speak, on account of the two Apostles
of Christ, are almost celestial, and Rome is the head
of all the churches of the world, saving the singular
prerogative of the place of the Lord's resurrection.
And so, as your honour is great with regard to the
dignity of your see, so is great care necessary lest you
lose your dignity on account of any perversity. . . .
For he is the true key-bearer of the heavens who,
through true knowledge, opens them to the worthy,
and closes them to the unworthy: otherwise he will be
able neither to open nor to close. . . . And since
these things are true and received without any contradiction by all who know the truth (although it is
known to all, and there is no one who does not know
how our Saviour gave to St. Peter the keys of the
kingdom of heaven, and how you—perhaps through
this—make for yourselves I know not what haughty
claim to greater authority and power in divine things
than others), know ye that your power will be less
with the Lord if ye even think this in your hearts;

for unity of faith in the whole world has made unity of power and prerogative."[1]

The same saint had written in a similar strain to Gregory the Great himself on another question,—that of the time of keeping Easter, on which the Irish Church long continued to differ from Rome and from the West in general. He had said, "Perhaps thou art content with the authority of thy predecessors, and especially of Pope Leo. Trust not, I pray thee, in such a question either to humility or gravity, which are often deceived. For in the problem before us a living dog is better than a dead lion." Observe the pun on the name of Leo. St. Columban's attitude on both these questions illustrates clearly how little the Celtic churches of the West were accustomed or disposed at that time to acknowledge papal claims. It is true that St. Columban's letters do not commit the Irish episcopate, since it was not from Ireland, but from Burgundy to Gregory, and from Lombardy to Boniface, after he had left his own country for missionary work, that he wrote. But the fact of Irish independence is otherwise evident. The bishops appear, indeed, to have afterwards consulted Gregory as to whether they should rebaptize reclaimed Nestorian heretics; to whom he replied, in accordance with the then and since established view, that the sacrament was not to be repeated, but only imposition of hands or chrism administered, in the case of such as had been already baptized in the name of the Trinity. He also stated

---

[1] The letter is given in Galland, *Biblioth. Patr.*, vii. 319.

at length and clearly the orthodox doctrine as against Nestorianism. But as we find from his letter that the emissary of the Irish had been at Jerusalem before coming to Rome, their application to the Pope cannot be construed as implying submission. They had probably sent only to learn the practice of the leading sees of Christendom; and their sending to Jerusalem before Rome agrees with what Columban says, in one of the letters above quoted, about the former see having a peculiar prerogative of sanctity even above the latter.[1]

In the same year (592) Gregory began to be occupied with troublesome matters of discipline in East Illyricum, the early subjection of which province to the spiritual supremacy of Rome was mentioned in our first chapter. There, therefore, he might fairly expect to be obeyed; as he was in some instances, but not in all. There were three cases. First, Hadrianus, bishop of Thebes, had been deposed by a synod under his metropolitan of Larissa; and the primate of Illyricum, John of Justiniana Prima, to whom the Emperor had referred the matter, had confirmed the sentence. But the deposed prelate appealed to Gregory, who summarily disallowed the whole proceedings as uncanonical, ordered the restoration of the appellant, exempted him in future from the jurisdiction of his metropolitan, excommunicated the primate for thirty days, threatening severer measures in case of disobedience to the authority of the Prince of the Apostles. No resistance is on record to this

---

[1] B. XI., Ind. iv., ep. 67.

assertion of power; nor in the second case, in which he ordered Natalis, metropolitan bishop of Salona, under pain of excommunication and eventual deposition, to reinstate his archdeacon Honoratus, whom he had deposed.[1]

The third case gave him much more trouble, inasmuch as the Emperor himself thought fit to interpose. On the death of Natalis of Salona, above named, Gregory recommended the aforesaid Archdeacon Honoratus for the see.[2] But one Maximus, alleged to be a man of scandalous life, and to have obtained his election by bribery, was elected without the Pope's leave or sanction. Gregory at once disallowed the proceeding, and wrote to the clergy of Salona forbidding them to choose a bishop without the knowledge and consent of the Apostolic See. But in the mean time the election had been confirmed by the Emperor, and the man ordained; on hearing which Gregory, with his accustomed deference to the imperial power, wrote a second letter, only suspending Maximus and his ordainers till he should be assured of the alleged imperial confirmation, but

---

[1] B. III., Ind. xi., epp. 6, 7.
[2] This Natalis of Salona was the prelate to whom the letter about addiction to banquets had been addressed. It may be that Honoratus, his archdeacon, had fallen into his bad graces for maintaining a stricter theory; possibly for telling the Pope of his superior's convivial tendencies. And Gregory's anxiety to promote Honoratus to the see may have been due to his desire to reform the laxity prevalent at Salona. Hence, as well as from his jealousy for the authority of Rome, may have arisen his soreness at being thwarted by the Emperor's interference.

summoning Maximus to give an account of himself at Rome. The suspension and summons were alike disregarded, and an order was obtained from the Emperor bidding the Pope give the bishop of Salona no further trouble. Gregory having in vain addressed a respectful but earnest remonstrance to the Emperor, saying that he would rather die than suffer any diminution of the authority of St. Peter's see, was obliged for the present to acquiesce. But before long he again summoned Maximus to Rome, on the ground of his alleged briberies, immoralities, and disregard of his former suspension. Maximus, relying on imperial support, again disregarded the summons, pleaded that, if he were liable to any charges, it was in his own province, not at Rome, that they ought to be inquired into, and sent to Constantinople counter accusations against Gregory himself. On this occasion the latter, as in other instances when he failed to move the Emperor, tried to get Constantina, the empress, on his side, pleading with her in an earnest letter, which affords a characteristic specimen of his style of writing to potentates. In it he says, "Obeying the commands of my lords, I allowed the ordination of this Maximus, though effected in presumptuous disregard of me or my representatives. But his other perversities—his corporal delinquencies which I have got knowledge of, his expenditure of church money to procure election, his continuing to celebrate mass though excommunicated—I cannot in conscience pass by. But my most serene lord has commanded me, before cognizance taken of these things, to receive him, when he comes to me, with honour. And it is indeed a very grave matter to honour a man of whom such things are alleged, before they have been fully sifted. And if the causes of bishops committed to my charge are taken out of my hands by my most pious lords, unhappy that I am, what shall I do? But that my bishops despise me, and resort against me to secular judges, thank God I attribute it to my sins. But I put my trust in Almighty God, that He will grant long life to my most pious lords, and deal with us, under your hand, not according to our sins, but according to the gifts of His grace. These things therefore I suggest to my most tranquil mistress, for I am not ignorant with what zeal for rectitude and justice the most upright conscience of your serenity is moved."[1] The case was not finally settled till seven years after its commencement. Seventeen letters remain, written by Gregory during its progress. At last the Emperor referred its adjudication to Maximinianus, bishop of Ravenna, and the result was that Maximus, having publicly begged the Pope's pardon, and having purged himself of the charge of simony by an oath taken at the tomb of St. Apollinaris at Ravenna, was accepted by Gregory as the lawful bishop of Salona. The whole case is interesting as illustrating Gregory's patient pertinacity in maintaining the claims of his see; but at the same time his habitual deference (under protest if necessary) to imperial authority, which his policy was to win by flattery rather than provoke by defiance. These characteristics are

[1] B. V., Ind. xiii., ep. 21.

observable throughout his career. He could, however, when strongly moved, speak his mind freely, and sometimes in a tone of courteous irony, to the Emperor himself, as instances presently to be adduced will show; and he never, even when open to the charge of adulation, compromised his own position in the ecclesiastical sphere.

The assertions of authority last recorded were in a region which had been for long under papal jurisdiction. In 593 a certain power of interference was claimed with the patriarch of Constantinople himself. But even in this large assumption Gregory did not in fact advance beyond the theory of some of his predecessors, to whom the view of an universal supremacy of St. Peter's see, with more or less distinctness, was already familiar. What he did was to seize all favourable opportunities of consolidating the system which the theory involved, and making it a reality where he could. It is, of course, to be remembered that the theory was never accepted by the Eastern Church. The circumstances were these: Two priests, John of Chalcedon and Anastasius of Isauria, had been condemned on a charge of heresy, and one of them beaten with cudgels under the patriarch of Constantinople, John the Faster. On hearing of this, Gregory wrote twice to the patriarch, in a tone of brotherly remonstrance, protesting against the introduction into the Church of a new and uncanonical punishment, urging that the two priests should be restored or judged canonically, and expressing his own readiness to receive them at Rome. The patriarch having in reply professed ignorance of the case referred to, Gregory wrote again in a tone of sarcasm, not without personality, which his professions of personal regard do not tend to soften. The style, it is to be remembered, was not usual with him; his letters generally, in accordance with his disposition, were very kind and courteous, though not unfrequently pervaded by delicate irony; it is his correspondence with and about his rival of Constantinople, whose ecclesiastical claims seem to have been a peculiarly sore point with him, that afford the most marked instance of a different tone. He wrote as follows: "Though consideration of the cause moves me, yet even charity now impels me to write, since, having written once and again to my most holy brother, I have received no reply from him. For some one else, a secular person, has addressed me in his name. And, indeed, if the letters received were his own, I shall have been much mistaken in him; for I expected from him something very different from what I have found. . . . . Your holy Fraternity has replied to me, as appears from the signature of the letter, that you were ignorant of what I had written about. At which reply I was mightily astonished, pondering with myself in silence, if what you say is true, what can be worse than that such things should be done against God's servants, and he who is over them should be ignorant? For what can be a shepherd's excuse if the wolf devours the sheep and the shepherd knows not? But, if your holiness did know both what subject I wrote about, and what had been done, either against John the Presbyter, or against Athanasius, monk of

Isauria and a presbyter, and has written to me, 'I know not,' what can I reply to this, since Scripture says, 'The mouth that lies slays the soul'? I ask, most holy brother, has all that great abstinence of yours come to this, that you would, by denial, conceal from your brother what you know to have been done? Would it not have been better that flesh should enter that mouth for food than that false words should come out of it for deceiving your neighbour, especially when the Truth says, 'Not that which goeth into the mouth defileth a man, but that which cometh out of the mouth, this defileth a man'"? The allusion here is, of course, to the patriarch's name of "the Faster," derived from his habits of abstinence. "But far be it from me to believe anything of the kind of your most holy heart. Those letters had your name appended to them, but I do not think they were yours. I wrote to the most blessed lord John, and I believe that that youngster, your familiar, has replied to me; he who has learnt nothing yet of God, who knows not the bowels of charity, who is accused by all of wickedness, who daily plots against the deaths of various persons by means of concealed wills, who neither fears God nor blushes in the sight of men. Believe me, most holy brother, if you have a real zeal for truth you must correct him in the first place, that by the example of those who are near to you those who are not near may be the better amended. Your holiness ought to direct him, not he influence your holiness. For I know that, if you listen to him, you will never have peace with your brethren. I exceedingly desire to have peace with all men, and especially with you, whom I greatly love, if only you are the same person as I once knew. But, if you set at naught the canons, I know not who you are. Yet so act, most holy and beloved brother, that we may mutually know each other; lest, if the old enemy cause scandal between us two, he cause the death of many by a most iniquitous victory. To speak plainly, if that youngster of whom I spoke had not reached at your side such a summit of depravity I should not have spoken about the canons, but have sent the complainants back to you, confident that you would do them justice. This is a new and unheard of way of preaching that exacts faith by blows. But I need not write at more length on this subject, since I am sending the deacon Sabinianus to you on my behalf, whom, unless you wish to be litigious with me, you will find prepared for everything that is just. I commend him to your Blessedness, that he at least may find that lord John whom I knew in the imperial city."[1]

The two priests did resort to Rome, in defiance of the patriarch, where they were absolved of heresy by Gregory after examination of their cause. As to the theory of his position on which he acted in this case, we find him in one of his letters writing thus: "With respect to the Constantinopolitan see, who doubts that it is subject to the Apostolical see?" and, "I know not what bishop is not subject to it, if fault be found in him."[2] A much more serious and prolonged

---

[1] B. III., Ind. xi., ep. 53.   [2] B. IX., Ind. ii., epp. 12, 59.

conflict with the see of Constantinople will come under our notice before long.

A different field of energy occupied Gregory in 594 and the following year, and one in which our highest admiration is due to him. He begins to stand out now as the prominent political figure of the day, as well as ecclesiastical. The Lombard invasion, and the distress in Italy thence ensuing, have been already spoken of. In the first years of his reign there had, however, been a temporary calm, owing to a treaty of peace that had been made between Romanus, the exarch of Ravenna, who represented the imperial power in Italy, and Agilulph, the Lombard king. The greater part of Italy was indeed now under Lombard sway. Antharis, the predecessor of Agilulph, had reduced Samnium and Beneventum, with most of Campania; he is said even to have advanced to Rhegium at the very toe of Italy, and riding into the sea, to have struck with his spear a pillar that stood there, saying "Thus far shall the bounds of the Lombards extend." Paul the Deacon, Gregory's biographer, speaks of a pillar still standing there in his day, and called "Antharis's Pillar." But the exarchate of Ravenna, the duchy of Rome, Naples, and some other maritime cities, were at this time unmolested. In the year, however, to which we have now come, Romanus, the exarch, in violation of the treaty, had seized the opportunity of the absence of Agilulph to invade the territory of the Lombards, and carry away the spoils of their cities to Ravenna. In reprisal, the king invaded the Exarchate, and remained for several months laying waste the country, and threatening Rome. The woful state of things at this crisis is pathetically described by Gregory in his letters, and also in some of the homilies on Ezekiel, which he preached during its continuance for the edification of the distressed Romans. In one homily he says, "What is there, I ask, in this world to take pleasure in? Everywhere we see sorrows, everywhere we hear groans. Cities are destroyed, castles ruined, fields laid waste, the land reduced to solitude. In the country is no inhabitant, scarcely any remain in the cities: yet even these small remnants of the human race are still daily and incessantly smitten. Some we see led into captivity, others maimed, others killed. What is there then to please us in this life, brethren? If we love such a world as this, we love not joys, but wounds. Nay, even she who once seemed to be the mistress of the world, Rome, what is she now? The Senate is no more, the people perishes; and even among the few that remain sorrows and groans are multiplied. But why say we these things of men, when, in increasing ruins, we see the very buildings destroyed? And what we say of the Roman city we know to be true of all the cities of the world. For some places are desolated by plague, some consumed with the sword, some tormented by famine, some swallowed by earthquakes. Let us despise then, with all our hearts, this well-nigh extinct present world. Let us end worldly desires, at least with the end of the world." In this rhetorical picture of exceptional and widespread woe we perceive the prevalent belief, often elsewhere expressed, that the end of all things was at hand. Again, at the conclusion of his last homily, he thus speaks: "Let no man blame me if henceforth I speak to you no more; for, as you all see, our tribulations have increased, we are everywhere surrounded by perils, everywhere is imminent danger of death: some return to us with their hands lopped off, others are reported to us as captured or slain. Now am I forced to refrain my tongue from exposition, for 'my soul is weary of life.' Let no one require of me now the study of sacred eloquence, for 'my harp is tuned to mourning, and my organ into the voice of them that weep'; 'for the voice of my groaning I forget to eat my bread.'" Such was Gregory's tone in the pulpit at this time. But it shows us only one side of the man. Most men who, at such a time, could thus feel and preach would have given themselves up only to resignation and prayer. Not so Gregory. He was constantly and efficiently active all the time in mitigating, as he could, the surrounding evils. He negotiated with the Lombard king, who was at length prevailed upon to conclude a special treaty of peace with himself, or a general one with the exarch, should the latter be willing to come to terms. Gregory urged him to do so, but being apparently interested in the continuance of the war for his own ends, he refused, and informed the Emperor that the Pope in his simplicity was being outwitted by the Lombard. Thereupon the Emperor addressed Gregory in a tone which, from the extant reply of the latter, seems to have been contemptuous and exasperating. "Your Piety, in its most serene command," so runs the courteous but cutting reply, "desirous of refuting me on certain matters, in sparing me has not spared me at all. For in using the polite word 'simplicity,' you really call me a fool. Simplicity may indeed in one sense be joined with prudence, according to the text, 'Be ye wise as serpents, but simple as doves.' But as, in your most serene commands, you represent me as deceived by the craftiness of Arnulph, denouncing me as simple without addition of prudence, I am undoubtedly called a fool. And indeed a fool I confess I am. For had I not been one, I should not have come to suffer what I do in this place among the swords of the Lombards." Perhaps he here alludes to the separate treaty of peace which he might have made with the enemy. He had been a fool, he would intimate, in expecting anything from the Exarch or the Emperor. He goes on, "But in that I am not believed in what I have stated about the disposition of Arnulph, and that credence is given to any one rather than me, I am also reprehended as having lied. But though I am not a priest" (he seems to refer here to something the Emperor had said) "I know it to be a grave injury to a priest to accuse him of falsehood. But indeed I could have borne contempt and derision in silence, but that my being accused of mendacity is the cause of the daily captivity of my country under the Lombard yoke; for, while I am in no respect believed, the strength of the enemy goes on increasing." After admonishing the Emperor at some length, and with considerable quiet sarcasm, on the respect due even from emperors to priests, in which he says even the heathen may afford an example, he enumerates existing grievances, which were,—his being deprived of the advantage of the peace which he had himself, without any detriment to the republic, made with the Lombards; then the withdrawal of soldiers from Rome so as to leave it without adequate defence; then the arrival of Agilulph at the gates, and the sight of Romans led away like dogs, with ropes about their necks, to be sold in France as slaves; then false charges of remissness brought against those who had, under great difficulties, defended the city, especially against Gregorius the prefect and Castorius the commandant, who, though they had neglected no duty, and had endured great hardship, had, after all this, been subjected to a commission of inquiry. He concludes the letter thus :—

"But, as to your Piety bidding me fear the terrible judgment of Almighty God, I beg you by the same Almighty God to do this no more; for we know not yet how any of us will stand there. And Paul, the excellent preacher, says, 'Judge nothing before the time, until the Lord come, who will both bring to light the hidden things of darkness and will make manifest the counsels of the hearts.' Yet this I briefly say, that I, unworthy and a sinner, presume more on the mercy of Jesus when He comes than on the justice of your Piety. And there are many things with respect to that judgment which men are ignorant of; for perchance what you praise He will reprehend, and what you reprehend He will praise. Wherefore, all these things being so uncertain, I return to tears only, praying that the same Almighty God may so rule our most pious master with His hand here, that in that terrible judgment He may find him free from all faults; and make me so to please men, if necessary, that I offend not eternal grace."[1]

Failing with the Emperor, he had recourse to the Empress, as in the matter of Maximus, writing to her at length, and detailing further the miserable state of things. He tells her that the ravages of the Lombards were not so bad as the cruelty and exactions of the imperial officers, who had been sent to defend the country; that the latter loaded the people with intolerable taxes, on pretence of raising funds for the war; that the Corsicans had in consequence been compelled to sell their children, and had gone over in great numbers to the enemy, leaving the island almost depopulated; that the real cause of the opposition raised to his own endeavours for peace by those who had the ear of the Emperor was a fear lest, with the ending of the war, the pretext for such exactions should cease. This appeal also had no result. But his unwearied efforts had better success with Theodelinda, the Lombard queen, who was a pious Catholic Christian, and with whom he kept up a correspondence, the important results of which will be hereafter seen. Through her, or at any rate partly through her intercession, Agilulph was, in 595, induced to withdraw his troops from the invaded territory.

In the same year (595) in which he thus obtained a temporary respite from worldly warfare, he began a memorable ecclesiastical battle, which lasted throughout his life. An Eastern judgment against an heretical priest had been sent to Rome, in which the

[1] B. V., Ind. xiii., Ep. 40.

patriarch of Constantinople was repeatedly entitled œcumenical, or universal, bishop. Now the title itself was not a new one. It had long been occasionally given to other patriarchs by flatterers; and already, before the time of Gregory, it had been especially conferred by the emperors Leo and Justinian on the patriarchs of Constantinople. Further, an Eastern synod held at Constantinople in 588 had confirmed it to the then patriarch, John the Faster, and his successors. But what in some circumstances might have been regarded as a mere title of honour was now open to a different interpretation. Hence even Pope Pelagius II. had protested against it when confirmed by the Eastern synod; and now that it came for the first time prominently under the notice of Gregory, it called forth his utmost indignation and resistance. He took it as expressing the supremacy of Constantinople rather than of Rome over the Church Universal; that of the prelate of the imperial city and imperial court rather than of the successor of St. Peter; and he represented it as implying a domination such as even Rome had no right to claim. It would be very unfair to attribute his remarkable vehemence of language and pertinacity of resistance on this occasion to mere offended pride or jealousy. According to his view, right or wrong, of the intended meaning of the title, a great principle may be said to have been at stake,—no less than that of spiritual prerogative as against imperialism. Constantinople had no claim to ascendency over the rest of the Church except that of being the see of the imperial city. On this ground, indeed, a rank of honour, second only to that of Rome, had been accorded to it by general councils; but this title seemed to Gregory to imply not only rank,—and that of the first, not the second order,—but also spiritual ascendency; and this claim really meant imperialism. He does not indeed rest his opposition on this ground, dwelling rather (perhaps from motives of policy) on the unlawfulness of any bishop claiming a universal episcopate; but, in estimating his conduct, we should not forget that in the claim, as he understood it, imperialism was involved. And it is easy to see what the practical result might have been, had a universal supremacy of Constantinople ever come to be generally recognized; which would have been in fact the domination over the Church of the corrupt imperial court itself rather than of its vassal patriarchs. On the other hand, the see of Rome in his eyes represented the Prince of the Apostles, and through him the apostolical commission, independent of all earthly powers. The validity of this assumption is a further question. It was at any rate then the tradition of the see, and the ground on which the popes went. In contending for the supremacy of Rome against Constantinople, Gregory might well feel himself to be contending for heavenly as against earthly jurisdiction, for Christ as against the world, for God as against Cæsar. But even for the successor of St. Peter he did not claim the title which was the subject of dispute. He repudiated it, by whomsoever assumed, as trenching on the rights of bishops in general, to all of whom the commission of Christ extended, though under the primacy of Peter. In one of his letters on the subject he does not even confine to his own see the representation of this primacy, allowing it to be shared by Antioch and Alexandria,—the former as having been St. Peter's first see before he went to Rome, the latter as having been founded by his disciple St. Mark. It may be difficult to reconcile this view with that at other times expressed, of the sole and peculiar supremacy of Rome, and he may possibly have been led to take it up, as he has been accused of doing, by his desire to enlist the other patriarchs in a common opposition to Constantinople. But entire consistency of view need not be looked for in one who wrote so much; and at any rate the view illustrates what was, after all, the important gist of the whole contest; viz., the assertion of the power of the keys derived from Christ, and not imperial patronage, as the ground and source of ecclesiastical jurisdiction. So far as his resolute struggle tended at all to establish this principle, and to save the Church from the possibility of being cramped and deadened by imperialism, he is entitled to the lasting gratitude of Christendom.

After receiving the document from Constantinople in which the offensive title repeatedly occurred, Gregory wrote at once to Sabinianus, his apocrisiarius, desiring him to protest against it, and also to the Patriarch himself, to the Emperor and Empress, inveighing against it in very strong language. He calls the title foolish, proud, pestiferous, profane, wicked, a diabolical usurpation; the ambition of any that assumed it he compares to that of Lucifer; he intimates that its assumption was a sign of the coming of the king of pride, that is, Antichrist. He takes it to mean the subjection of all bishops to one, whereas St. Paul was horror-struck at the idea of the members of Christ being subordinated to any single headship except His, saying, "Was Paul crucified for you? &c." Nay even Peter, to whom were given the keys of the kingdom of Heaven, and to whom, as Prince of the Apostles, the care of the whole Church was committed, is nowhere called "Universal Apostle." If any could take the title, it would be St. Peter's successor; but all popes had refused it, lest, by taking this singular honour to themselves, they should deprive all priests of the honour due to them. It had been offered to the Pope by the Council of Chalcedon, but persistently declined. The only foundation for this last allegation, which Gregory repeatedly made, seems to be that Pope Leo's representative Paschasius had at Chalcedon applied the title to the Pope, and that the bishops present had not objected.

If, he asks, the whole Church had in times past depended on one, and that one the Patriarch, what would have become of it when patriarchs had been heretics, or even heresiarchs? It may be observed, that this last argument tells equally (unless we assume the more recent theory of personal infallibility) against the view which binds the whole Church to papal teaching "ex cathedrâ." Indeed, Gregory's whole position against the Constantinopolitan patriarch may be fairly adduced (notwithstanding his undoubted maintenance of a universal primacy and authority, in some sense, belonging to St. Peter's chair) as against the more advanced theory of the popedom, such as has in our own days been authoritatively promulged.

Gregory's feeling of personal soreness against John the Faster, which was observable in his former correspondence with him, appears also on this occasion. In his long letter to him, though it is tempered by expressions of courtesy and affection, there is no lack of strong language. But it seems that he had restrained himself from saying all that was in his mind. For, in writing at the same time to his apocrisiarius Sabinianus, he tells him that his letter to the Patriarch, which was to be given him then, was mixed with blandishments, out of consideration for the Emperor, but that he intended to write him another, such as "his pride would not rejoice in." And in his letter to the Emperor there are again sarcastic allusions to John's asceticism. Attributing the successes of the enemies of the empire to the iniquities and presumption of the clergy, he says, again alluding to the Patriarch's ascetic reputation, "Our bones are attenuated by fasts, and our hearts swell with pride: our body is clothed in vile raiment, and in the elation of our heart we surpass the purple: we lie in ashes, and we mind high things: teachers of humility, but examples of pride, we hide the teeth of wolves with a sheep's face." He goes on to implore the Emperor to restrain this crying evil by the chains of his august authority, since "the pious laws of the empire, the venerable synods, the commands of Christ Himself, are set at naught by the invention of a proud and pompous title."[1]

Neither his letters nor his withdrawal of Sabinianus from communion with the Patriarch having had any effect at Constantinople, he addressed himself to the other patriarchs,—to Eulogius of Alexandria, and Anastasius of Antioch, with the view of obtaining their concurrence in his protest; representing the purpose of their brother of Constantinople as being that of degrading them, and usurping to himself all ecclesiastical power. But they were not thus moved to action: they seem to have treated the title as one of honour only, and not of the importance assigned to it by their correspondent.

In the year 596 John the Faster died, and was succeeded by Cyriacus. Gregory renewed his protest. He directed his apocrisiarius at Constantinople to demand of the new patriarch, as a condition of intercommunion, the renunciation of the "proud and pestiferous title," which his predecessor had impiously assumed. Cyriacus sent a nuncio to Rome to try to arrange matters. But Gregory was resolute. He says, in a letter to the Patriarch on this occasion: "I confidently say, that whoever calls himself universal priest, or desires in his elation to be called so, is the forerunner of Antichrist." He also wrote again to the Emperor on the subject, and to the two patriarchs of Antioch and Alexandria, the former of whom seems still to have disapproved of his persistence on the question. For to him Gregory

---

[1] B. V., Ind. xiii., Epp. 18, 19, 20, 21.

now wrote, after acknowledging and disclaiming the personal compliments with which his correspondent had begun his letter: "But your Holiness, I perceive, by the words of sweetness at the beginning of your letter and by what follows after, has wished it to be like a bee that carries both honey and a sting, satiating me with the honey and then piercing me with the sting. I am thus led to meditate on the words of Solomon, 'Better are the wounds of a friend than the kisses of an enemy.' For, as to your saying that I ought not to give occasion of scandal for no cause at all, this is what our most pious master (for whose life we ought continually to pray) has repeatedly written to me; and what he says out of power, I know that you say out of love. Nor do I wonder that you have inserted imperial words in your letter, since between power and love there is a close relationship. For both command in a princely way; both speak authoritatively." The delicate tone of irony not seldom used by Gregory is perceptible in this letter, at the conclusion of which he maintains that the title on account of which he is accused of disturbing the peace of the Church, is no mere idle phrase, but one carrying an important meaning.[1] He got more sympathy from the Alexandrian patriarch, Eulogius, who, though there is no evidence of his having joined in the desired protest, wrote, at any rate, acknowledging the pre-eminent dignity of St. Peter's see. It was in reply to this letter that Gregory expressed the peculiar view of the Apostle's

[1] B. VII., Ind. xv., Ep. 46.

primacy being shared by three sees, which has been above alluded to. The words are too remarkable to be left unquoted. "All that you have said I willingly accept, because he who has spoken to me of the chair of St. Peter occupies it himself. And, though special honour to myself by no means delights me, yet I am greatly rejoiced, inasmuch as what you, most holy ones, have bestowed on me you have given to yourselves. For who knows not that the holy Church was made firm in the solidity of the Prince of the Apostles, whose name expressed the firmness of his mind? .... Wherefore, though there were many Apostles, yet the see of the Prince of the Apostles alone has acquired a principality of authority, which is the see of one only, though in three places. For he himself exalted the see in which he deigned to rest and to end his present life. He himself adorned the see to which he sent his disciple as Evangelist. He himself established the see in which he sat for seven years. Since, then, the see is one and of one, over which by divine authority three bishops now preside, whatever good I hear of you I impute to myself. If you believe anything good of me, impute this to your own merits; because we are one in Him who said, 'That they all may be one, as thou, Father, art in Me, and I in Thee, that they all may be one in us.'"[1] But when Eulogius, in return for this exaltation of his own see, afterwards addressed Gregory as "Universal Pope," he strongly repudiated the title, saying, "I have said that neither to me nor to

[1] B. VII., Ind. xv., Ep. 46.

any one else ought you to write anything of the kind: and lo! in the preface of your letter you apply to me, who prohibited it, the proud title of Universal Pope; which thing I beg your most sweet Holiness to do no more, because what is given to others beyond what reason requires is subtracted from you. I do not esteem that an honour by which I know my brethren lose their honour. My honour is that of the Universal Church. I am then truly honoured when all and each are allowed the honour that is due to them. For, if your Holiness calls me Universal Pope, you deny yourself to be that which you call me universally. But no more of this: away with words which inflate pride and wound charity!" He even objects to the expression, "as thou hast commanded," which had occurred in his correspondent's letter. "Which word, commanded, I pray you let me hear no more; for I know what I am, and what you are: in position you are my brethen, in manners you are my fathers. I did not, therefore, command, but desired only to indicate what seemed to me expedient."[1] We have here the unusual case of a pope disclaiming, rather than claiming authority, refusing, in fact, to accept as much as was freely offered, and putting two at least of his brethren on an entire equality with himself.

Subsequently (A.D. 600) we find him writing to the same Eulogius, with reference to some form of heresy which the Alexandrian patriarch had condemned, but on which he had desired his opinion, in the following

[1] B. VIII., Ind. i., Ep. 30.

high-flown terms :—"In the letter of my most holy brother I recognize the voice of the venerable fathers whom I love so much. Wherefore praise and glory in the highest be to Him by whose gift the voice of Mark still cries aloud in the see of Peter, and by the effusion of whose spirit, when the priest enters into the investigation of mysteries, that is, into the Holy of Holies, spiritual bells from the word of preaching resound in holy Church as in the Tabernacle. But we implore Almighty God to preserve you long in this life, that from the organ of God, which you are, the voice of truth may resound more widely. But for me intercede, I pray you, that the way of my pilgrimage, which has grown so rough to me, may be speedily ended; so that by your merits, as I cannot by my own, I may attain to the promises of our eternal country, and rejoice with the citizens of heaven."[1]

A doubt may indeed well be felt whether, but for his anxiety to enlist the great patriarchs against Constantinople, he would have expressed himself as he did. But such was his language on this occasion; and it remains for the consideration of modern ultramontanists. All his efforts to procure the renunciation of the title proving entirely without effect at Constantinople, he was obliged to content himself with protest, which, however, had its effect afterwards, though he did not live to see it. It is supposed to have been by way of contrast to the assumption of his rival that he afterwards constantly styled himself in his letters, "Servant of the servants of God,"

[1] B. X., Ind. iii., Ep. 35.

though he had previously sometimes used the expression. This, as is well known, has since been the formula used by the popes of themselves.

During the continuance of this ecclesiastical struggle he was again involved in mundane trouble, owing to the Lombard king, provoked by the Exarch's continued rejection of overtures, having towards the close of 596 again invaded the Exarchate, and threatened to besiege Rome. Gregory renewed his patriotic efforts, and, as before, stands out as the single champion, unassisted by exarch or emperor. He did more than complain, remonstrate, and negociate. The direction even of military operations, in a crisis like this, he did not consider inconsistent with his sacred office, for we find him in 599 directing Januarius, bishop of Cagliari, to cause his city and other places to be more strongly fortified and replenished against a possible hostile attack; as on a former occasion (when in 592 a truce with the Lombard king was being negotiated) he had enjoined the military officers in command to be ready, "as became brave men," to attack Agilulph in the rear, and plunder his territory, should he still move towards Ravenna or Rome; and had written to the soldiera at Naples bidding them yield entire obedience to the tribune whom he had sent to defend their city.[1] He also exerted himself to raise funds, by appeals in various quarters, for relief of distress and redemption of captives; and he authorized bishops to sell or pledge the sacred vessels of their churches for the

[1] B. IX., Ind. ii., Ep .7; B. II., Ind. x., Epp. 3, 29, 30, 31.

purpose. He has been accused, and not without some grounds, of superstitious devotion. Here, however, we have evidence of his recognition of the paramount claims of humanity; of his placing mercy above sacrifice. His activity in these respects, with the cause for it, lasted through several years, simultaneously with work of other kinds, which will be noticed in due order. Suffice it to say that at length, in the year 600, when he had for two years been confined to his bed by illness, and again, it would seem, through the influence of Queen Theodelinda, he succeeded in concluding a truce with the Lombards from September to the April of the following year; and to add that, if his success in this protracted struggle amounted after all only to occasional truces with the enemy, and mitigation of distress through charity, and through Christian influences brought to bear on the invaders, the blame rests on the Emperor and his representatives, not on him. Whatever good was done was due to him, and him alone.

CHAPTER V.

The Mission to England—Story of the Slaves in the Roman Forum—State of the Church in France—Correspondence with Brunehild—Pall sent to Virgilius—Reforms urged—Candidus sent—Cyriacus—A General Synod desired—Failure to obtain one—Eventual results—Augustine despatched to England—His success—His alleged Miracles—His questions and the replies to them—Scheme for the English Church—Letter to Mellitus—Letters to Bertha and Ethelbert—The British Christians—The Lombards—Theodelinda—Conversion of Agilulph (596—601).

THE year 596 is memorable as the date of the inauguration of Gregory's famous mission to England; the foundation of the Christianity of our Teutonic ancestors, as distinct from the earlier conversion of the Celtic inhabitants of the British islands. Before his accession, during his monastic life, he had conceived the desire of evangelizing in person the heathen invaders of Britain. The story about the slaves in the Roman market-place has been often told. His biographer, John the Deacon, gives it thus: Observing one day some boys with fair complexions, comely faces, and bright flowing hair, exposed for sale, he asked whence they came. Being told "from Britain," he inquired whether the inhabitants of that island were Christians or pagans. Learning that they were pagans, he heaved long sighs, and said, "Alas that men of such lucid countenance should be possessed by the author of darkness, and that such grace of form should hide minds void of grace within!" Being told further, in answer to his inquiries, that they were called Angli, "Well so called," said he, "for they have angelic faces, and should be coheirs in heaven with angels. What is the name of the province from which they come?" Being told that it was Deira, "Right again," was his reply, "From the wrath of God (*de ira Dei*) are they rescued, and called to the mercy of Christ." Lastly, on hearing that the king of that province was called Aella, he exclaimed, "Alleluiah! the praise of God the Creator must be sung in those parts."

As to the period of his monastic life in which the incident occurred his biographers differ. John the Deacon, writing in the 9th century, places it before his mission to Constantinople; Paul the Deacon, writing in the previous century, after his return. But they agree as to the facts as above related, and as to what immediately followed. He went at once (we are told) to the Pope (Benedict according to John, Pelagius according to Paul), and implored leave to attempt in person the conversion of the English, which was reluctantly granted He set out without delay, accompanied by some of his monks, without the knowledge of the Roman people. But they, when his departure became known, were greatly perturbed, and, dividing themselves into three companies, assailed the Pope as he went to church, crying "with a terrible voice," "Ah! what hast thou done? Thou hast offended St. Peter, thou has destroyed Rome, since thou hast sent away Gregory!"

Whereupon the Pope, greatly alarmed, sent with all possible speed to recall him to Rome. He meanwhile had already made a three days' journey, and was reading at midday while his companions rested, when a locust settled on his book. Being still, it seems, in a vein for playing on words, he took this as an omen, and, calling his friends, said to them, "*Locusta* signifies *loco sta* (stay where you are), and portends that we are not allowed to continue our journey; but rise and saddle the beasts, and let us haste on our way as far as we may." As he spoke, the messengers arrived, their horses foaming and tired, and took him back to Rome. In the earlier part of 596, when he had been for six years Pope, we find the first evidence of his still having his project for the conversion of England at heart. For he wrote at that time to Candidus, a priest sent to superintend the papal patrimony in Gaul, directing him to use part of the revenue in the purchase of English youths, of the age of 17 or 18 years, to be educated in monasteries, intending them, we may suppose, as missionaries to their own countrymen.[1] The long-cherished design he at length carried out in earnest, through the mission of the monk Augustine later in the same year.

Before giving an account of this important mission, some notice of his relations to the Church in France, through which country the mission passed, and to the magnates of which it was commended, may be here suitably introduced. The Franks had, since 486, been masters of the greatest part of Gaul. The

[1] B. VI., Ind. xiv., Ep. 7.

conversion of Clovis, king of the Salian Franks, to Catholic Christianity, about the year 496, has been alluded to in our first chapter. Subsequent conquests by him and his descendants had subjected to the Frank empire not only France, but the western and central parts of Germany, besides Bavaria, Burgundy, and perhaps Swabia. The Catholicity of the princes of the house of Clovis, commonly called the Merovingian dynasty, led them to support and patronize the Church that had from early times been founded in Roman Gaul, and to endow it richly, while they took measures to extirpate as they could all lingering heathenism. But their patronage involved domination. While they valued the support and the prayers of bishops and abbats, and enlarged the powers of the former, they regarded them as vassals with respect to their temporalities; they allowed no bishop to be elected without their own confirmation, and usually made the appointments themselves, often nominating laymen out of favouritism, or selling the appointment to the highest bidder; no synods could assemble without their leave; and altogether they exercised a large control, and sort of feudal suzerainty, over the Church which they supported. The authority of the Bishop of Rome was acknowledged and accepted by them, but he could ordinarily exert but little direct control, and was dependent for its exercise on the royal pleasure. Further, the character of these princes, with regard both to immorality and violent atrocities, was generally very bad, notwithstanding their Christianity: the records of their period reveal little more than a succession of crimes. Such was the state of things with which Gregory had to deal; and he omitted no opportunity of influence, carrying on a correspondence with the several reigning sovereigns, and with prelates in their dominions. His letters to the former were conceived with characteristic prudence. To have dictated, or addressed them in a tone of authority, might have defeated his end; he therefore uses the language of courteous exhortation and of compliment, recognizing their authority over their subjects, ecclesiastical as well as lay, and endeavouring to utilize the royal power for ecclesiastical purposes. His tone in addressing one of these potentates especially, Brunehild (or Brunhaut), has been charged against him as an instance of culpable adulation, considering the character of the person addressed. She governed Austrasia, *i.e.* the eastern or German part of the empire, during the minority of her son Childebert II., and was again the virtual ruler of both Austrasia and Burgundy, when on the death of Childebert (596) his two sons, Dielbert and Dietrich, had these kingdoms respectively assigned to them. It is true that this princess has had advocates in modern times, who have endeavoured to vindicate her from the charge of crimes of peculiar magnitude; but the general verdict of historians is against her.[1] It was, indeed, after Gregory's death that her profligate conduct called forth the strong reproof of St. Columban, who was then in Burgundy, for which he incurred her bitter enmity, and was banished the kingdom after im-

---

[1] *See* Hallam's "Middle Ages," vol. i. p. 4.

prisonment. And it is true that Gregory of Tours commends her character, as well as her abilities, in the earlier years of her life. But it is conceived that Gregory must in his time have known too well what she was at the time when he wrote to justify such addresses as, for instance, "We give thanks to Almighty God, who, among the other gifts of His goodness bestowed on your excellency, has so filled you with love of the Christian religion that whatever you know to be conducive to the propagation of the faith you cease not to effect with devout mind and pious zeal."[1] Again: "Among your other excellencies this is chief, that, in the midst of the waves of this world which are wont to perturb the minds of rulers, you so apply your heart to the love of divine worship as if no other care troubled you. Hence we declare the nation of the Franks to be happy beyond all other nations in being blessed with a queen so endowed with all good gifts."[2] He had regard, doubtless, in such praises, to her support of the Church and the Catholic faith, and probably to her outward acts of devotion: whatever crimes she might be guilty of had either not reached his ears, or were judiciously ignored by him, according to his policy (which was one of his characteristics) of conciliating the powers of the world by deference and compliment, if he could so enlist them in the cause of good. Another point to be noted in this regard is his habit of thus gaining influence especially over royal ladies, the possibilities of whose influence on

[1] B. XI., Ind. iv., Ep. 62.   [2] B. XIII., Ind. vi., Ep. 6.

others he was fully alive to. He knew how Clotilda had been the means of converting Clovis to Catholicity; and he felt that female influence might be in other cases powerful. Nor were his anticipations unfulfilled. Hence his continued and affectionate correspondence with the Lombard Theodelinda, as well as with the less worthy Brunehild, his letters to the Empress Constantina, and afterwards, as will be seen, to Bertha, queen of Kent, and Leontia, the wife of the Emperor Phocas. If, in the case of Brunehild, and still more in his addresses to Phocas and Leontia, which will be noticed afterwards, he is liable to the charge of adulating those whom he must have known to be unworthy, it was, we may suppose, that in such cases the wisdom of the serpent was in excess of the simplicity of the dove; and, with regard to Brunehild, it is to be remembered, that dealing with the Frank potentates was a critical matter, in which adroit diplomacy was required.

It was in 595, when his relations with Constantinople and the Eastern Church were at the worst, that he seized an opportunity of strengthening his connection with the Church in the Frank dominions, a connection of more importance in its ultimate results than any with the waning empire of the Cæsars. In this year King Childebert sent to request the pallium for Virgilius, bishop of Arles. This voluntary demand for a renewal of the old dependence of the see of Arles, and through it of the Church in Gaul, on the Roman see, was most welcome to Gregory. He at once complied, sending at the same time a cordial letter to Childebert, constituting the bishop of Arles his vicar, "according to ancient custom and the desire of your excellency," and desiring the king in return to support the authority of Virgilius, and "for the sake of God and St. Peter," to cause the ordinances of Rome to be observed throughout his kingdom, "so far (he prudently adds) as they fall in with the opinion of your laudable excellency." He took the opportunity also of speaking strongly against the promotion of laymen to bishoprics, and against the simony, said to be prevalent in France, and implored the king, as he loved his own salvation, to rectify such abuses. He wrote also to Virgilius, and to all the bishops of Childebert's kingdom, exhorting the latter to obedience, and the former to zeal, combined with humility and prudence. He is directed to assemble synods of bishops as occasion might require, and to refer any matter on which they could not agree to Rome. Especially he is urged to use his utmost endeavours to obtain from the king the utter extirpation of the crying evils of simony and the promotion of laymen. Against the first of these abuses he is unremitting in his denunciations, comparing it to that of the money-changers in the Temple: of the second he uses the following illustrations: "We know that newly-built walls do not receive the weight of a roof till they have had time to dry, lest, if they are burdened before being solidified, the whole fabric should fall to the ground. And when we cut trees for a building, we wait for the moisture of their viridity to be dried out, lest, if the weight of the building be imposed on them while yet fresh, they be bent from their very newness, and break down the more speedily from being immaturely raised on high. Why, then, is not the same principle nicely observed in dealing with men, which is so carefully considered in the case of wood and stone?"[1] In the following year (596) he sent the priest Candidus (as has been already mentioned) for the management of the patrimony in Gaul, with letters of commendation to the royal potentates, probably intending him to be (as such functionaries were elsewhere) his general agent and informant with respect to Church affairs. He continued to write urgently to Brunehild and Childebert, and especially to the former, as well as to bishops, pressing on them the reform of the still-continued abuses before complained of, the correction of clerical immorality, the suppression of heathenism, and the convening of a general synod for the purposes in view. He endeavoured to move the royal potentates to action by appeals to their sense of temporal and spiritual advantage, as well as by flattering phrases, saying, for instance, on one occasion to Brunehild, "May your Excellency deign to comply willingly with what we desire, that the blessed Peter, the prince of apostles, to whom the power of binding and loosing has been given by Christ, may both grant to your Excellency to have joy in your offspring here, and to be found, after a course of many years, absolved from all evils before the face of the Eternal Judge." In 599 he sent Cyriacus, abbat of the monastery of St. Andrew's at Rome, commissioned to bring about the assembly of the long-desired synod, which was to be presided over by Syagrius, bishop of

---

[1] B. V., Ind. xiii., Epp. 53, 54, 55.

Autun, to whom, at Brunehild's request, he had already sent the pallium, and who was apparently selected as likely to have influence with the ruling powers. He renewed at the same time his urgent appeals to Brunehild and her royal grandsons, and to the bishops in general.[1] The synod, however, never assembled. The evils to be remedied were too closely bound up with worldly interests, and the Frank rulers were still too independent of spiritual domination, for Gregory to realize at that time the plans for organization and reform which he had so much at heart. But his labours were not without important fruits: they established the theory of the primacy of Rome over the Church of the rising Empire of the West, and paved the way for the ecclesiastical independence and papal supremacy of a later age. Not least important among his measures towards this end—important beyond the range of his foresight at the time—was the mission which will come next under our review, undertaken at the time with no ulterior purpose, but out of motives of pure philanthropy—the mission through France to England. For the closer dependence of the English Church on Rome, to whom it owed its birth, could not but have an influence on the churches of the Continent; and especially it was the English Boniface, than whom the popes had never a more devoted son, who afterwards brought the remaining heathen into the fold, and strengthened the Roman obedience among the German races.

The establishment of the relations above detailed

---

[1] B. IX., Ind. ii., Epp. 105, 106, 108, 114 117.

with the Church and rulers of France probably suggested to Gregory, in 596, that circumstances were now favourable for speeding a mission through the country, so as to realize his old design of the evangelization of England, especially as a daughter of the Frank king Charibert had now been married to King Ethelbert of Kent, and had already her church and priest in his heathen kingdom, with the free exercise of her own religion. From what has been said above, it is evident that in this last circumstance Gregory could perceive a peculiarly hopeful opening.

Augustine, prior of St. Andrew's monastery, of which Gregory had been founder and abbat, was selected as the head of the mission, being intended also as bishop in case of its success. Other monks were associated with him, and he was instructed to avail himself also of the services of any clergy in Gaul whom he might approve of, if willing to join him. For the furtherance of this end, and by way of commending the mission generally to royal favour, he charged them with letters to the kings Theodoric (or Thierri) and Theodebert, and to Queen Brunehild, and also to Virgilius, bishop of Arles (whom he had constituted, as has been already seen, his legate in Gaul), and to other bishops and influential persons. After temporary delay, owing to Augustine having turned faint-hearted on the road, and returned to Rome to beg the Pope to give up his project, on which he had been sent back with letters of encouragement to his colleagues,—the missionaries landed at length on the isle of Thanet, were admitted into Canterbury, were favourably received by King

Ethelbert, and thus commenced their labours. It does not fall within the scope of this life to pursue the history of the mission; but it is of importance for the illustration of our hero's character, to notice particularly the part he took in its direction and support.

After the baptism of Ethelbert, the general conversion of his subjects in Kent, who soon followed the example of their king, and the consecration of Augustine as bishop by the Bishop of Arles, according to Gregory's original intention in the event of success, the cheering news was sent to Rome through Laurentius the priest, and Peter the monk, who were despatched for the purpose. At the same time, Gregory's directions were requested on a number of questions on which Augustine had doubt. This request elicited a long reply, which is of peculiar interest. In the first place, we find a letter of congratulation to Augustine, in which, while thanks are returned to Heaven for the wonderful success reported, he is warned against personal elation on the ground of the miracles which had accompanied his preaching. He is reminded of the judgment on Moses for his sin when he brought water out of the rock, and of our Lord's reply to His disciples when they reported that even the devils were subject to them; and fear is expressed lest he should think more of his own glory than of his election and of the general salvation of souls. Now the miracles of Augustine are alluded to as known facts, about which there was no doubt; and the question naturally arises, what view we are to take of them. St. Gregory has been charged with superstition, with silly credulity, or with a spice of knavery, for giving such ready credence, or affecting to do so, not only to the reported miracles of Augustine, but also to countless others, recorded especially in his Book of Dialogues. The Protestant Mosheim speaks of him as combining with "a sound and penetrating judgment" in some cases "the most shameful and superstitious weakness," and calls him "this good but silly pontiff." Gibbon, though on the whole laudatory, describes him as "a singular mixture" of "simplicity and cunning," of "sense and superstition"; and in his refined sneering tone remarks, "the credulity, or the prudence, of Gregory was always disposed to confirm the truths of religion by the evidence of ghosts, miracles, and resurrections." But do not such censures betray a want of comprehension of him and of his age? Nothing is less philosophical than to judge men of the past by the standard of ideas current in one's own day. First, we may observe that to thorough believers in the miracles of the New Testament their continuance or recurrence cannot appear *à priori* improbable. To them it is simply a question of evidence whether they did continue or not. To us the evidence of their continuance appears manifestly insufficient; but it is not so much the lack of evidence as the widespread theory of our day adverse to all miracles whatever (which in so many minds is undermining faith even in those of the Biblical record) that is at the bottom of the utterly contemptuous rejection of all later ones, which is now thought the mark of an enlightened mind. In estimating, therefore, the mental attitude of Gregory and others of his age, we must dismiss from our minds modern scientific notions about the fixed uniformity of the laws of nature, which require even Scriptural miracles to be accounted and apologized for as something quite exceptional. In that earlier age such notions were unknown to the believing Christian. The supernatual order of things, testified to by evangelists and apostles, was attended to him by no intellectual difficulties, and its continuance seemed to him more likely than its sudden cessation. Nor was it an age of scientific sifting of evidence: the proofs demanded by modern inductive science were not demanded then; little was required to satisfy people that what was thought likely to happen had actually happened. Further, the infectious enthusiasm of the monastic movement had introduced visions and marvels into the general world of thought; the air was full of them, and it would be thought impious to impugn the experience of those who were accounted saints. The consequence was, that, wherever there were saintly monks and religious fervour, miraculous incidents were both looked for and perceived. There may doubtless have been imposture in some cases, since where there is a general demand for anything in excess of the supply, people will usually be found to manufacture counterfeits. But to attribute the main supply to monastic knavery is to read the records of the period with a very prejudiced and undiscerning eye. Most of the incidents on record, supposed to be miraculous, may now be accounted for by the prevalent state of feeling and expectancy above described, under which a miraculous colour could be given to remarkable natural events, objective reality would be assigned to mental impressions, and exaggeration in accordance with preconceived ideas would rapidly affect narratives. Nor ought we to leave out of our account the remarkable and abnormal phenomena that are known actually to occur—in the way, for instance, of recovery from disease,—where there is unusually strong faith, and especially where crowds are actuated by infectious enthusiasm. Such, then, seems to be the most probable explanation of the wonders spoken of; and, if so, it is evident that Gregory cannot be justly accused of either silliness or insincerity in avowing his full belief in their supernatural character. Being a fervently religious man of the age he lived in, he could hardly help believing. Disbelief in him would have been an anachronism. And all must allow that, in his letter to Augustine, he at any rate assigns to such wonders their true value, and does not exaggerate their importance. "Not all the elect," he writes, " work miracles, and yet the names of all of them are written in heaven. And the disciples of truth should have joy in that good only which they have in common with all, and in which there will be no end of their joy." Again, "Through signs the gain of souls is be sought, and His glory by whose power the very signs are wrought. But the Lord hath given us one sign in which we may exceedingly rejoice, and recognize the glory of election in ourselves, saying, 'In this shall it be known that ye are My disciples, if ye have love one to another.' Which sign the prophet required when he said, 'Show me, Lord, a sign for good, that they which hate me may see it and be confounded.'"

The questions of Augustine were eleven in number.

The chief ones follow, with summaries of the answers to them:—

I. How ought bishops to live with their clergy, and how ought the offerings of the faithful at the altar to be distributed? *Answer:* It is the custom of the Apostolic See to instruct all bishops to make a fourfold division of the revenue accruing to them: for the maintenance of their own households and of hospitality; for the clergy; for the poor; and for repairing churches. But, since you, being a monk, ought not to live apart from your clergy, you must in England return to the primitive system of having all things in common.

II. May clerks who cannot contain be allowed to marry; and, if they marry, ought they to return to the world? *Answer:* Clerks not in holy orders may marry, if they have not a gift for celibacy, and receive their stipends separately, continuing still under ecclesiastical rule and supervision.

III. There being but one faith, what is to be done with regard to the great difference of customs in different churches? The churches of Gaul, for instance, celebrate mass differently from the Roman Church. *Answer:* You are familiar with the custom of the Roman Church in which you have been nurtured; but I desire you to select diligently whatever things you find most pleasing to Almighty God, pious, religious, and right in all churches, and collecting them as it were into a bundle, introduce them into the custom of the infant Church of England. For things are not to be loved for places, but places for the good things found in them.

IV. How are robbers of churches to be dealt with? *Answer:* Differently in different cases. For some steal to supply want, others though not in need. Wherefore some are to be punished by fines, others by stripes; and some more severely than others. But even when the treatment is somewhat severe, it should be administered with charity; in the spirit in which good fathers correct their children, whom they still intend to make their heirs. And in no case must more than restitution of what was stolen be demanded; for God forbid that the Church should make worldly profit out of her losses.

V. May two brothers marry two sisters? *Answer:* Yes. There is no prohibition of such marriages in Scripture.

VI. Within what degree of consanguinity may marriage be allowed? *Answer:* The Roman civil law allows marriage of first cousins. But it is found to have bad results with regard to offspring; and the general rule of Scripture is against it. Marriage, then, within the third or fourth degree, is to be prohibited: and it is manifestly impious for a man to marry his stepmother.

VII. Should converts who have married within the prohibited degrees be separated and denied communion? *Answer:* Those who have so married while still in heathenism are to be warned to abstain from intercourse lest they incur eternal torments for temporal enjoyment. But they are not on this account to be debarred from communion. For the Church in some cases best suppresses evils by forbearance and toleration. But, after baptism, such marriages are to be forbidden under pain of privation of communion.

VIII. May a bishop ever be ordained by a single bishop, when others cannot easily be got together? *Answer:* Being so far the only bishop in England, you must of necessity ordain alone, unless bishops from Gaul should ever come to you, in which case they must assist. But I desire you to ordain bishops in England at no great distance from each other, so that in future three or four may always be assembled for the ordination of others.

IX. How are we to deal with the bishops of Gaul and Britain? *Answer:* I give you no authority over the bishops of Gaul, who have of old been subject to the Metropolitan of Arles. Should you, however, be in Gaul, and find the Bishop of Arles remiss in discipline, you may endeavour to inflame his zeal by gentle persuasion and example, taking care not to assume authority. Over all British bishops we give you full authority.

The remaining questions refer mainly to certain causes of impurity, real or supposed; as to whether people should be debarred on account of them from church or communion. Gregory answers variously. As to many of them he says that, being natural and unavoidable, or falling under no distinct law of prohibition, they are not to exclude from church privileges, though persons are not blamed who on such grounds, out of reverence, absent themselves. The whole series of replies is a remarkable instance of clearness and readiness of judgment, and also of moderation and good sense. Had Augustine, in his dealings with the British bishops, taken more heed to the view expressed of the variability of rites and customs, and acted generally more in his master's spirit of accommodation and forbearance than Bede represents him to have done, it may be that the ancient British Church might have submitted to his control, and the long schism that ensued been avoided.

Gregory sent also at this time to Augustine a pall, in token of metropolitan jurisdiction, together with books, vestments, sacred vessels, ornaments and relics, for the use of churches, and a reinforcement of missionaries; among whom were Justus, Paulinus, and Rufinianus. Further, he gave him a sketch of his intended organization of the English Church, which was eventually carried out in its main features, and has continued to our own day, though Canterbury, as the original seat of the mission, never came to be superseded by London, as was at first intended. According to this scheme, there were to be two metropolitan sees, in the north and the south, at London and York, each with twelve suffragans under them: York was to be subject to London during Augustine's life, but independent after his death, while to him were to be subjected all existing British bishops. This last provision failed, as is well known, through the Britons refusing to admit the authoritative claims, asserted apparently with injudicious imperiousness, of the new emissary of Rome. Afterwards to the abbat Mellitus, who had also been sent from Rome, Gregory addressed a remarkable letter, singular for its spirit of prudent accommodation. Mellitus, being still in France, is instructed to warn Augustine, on his arrival in England, not to destroy the heathen temples, but to consecrate them for Christian use by holy water, erection of altars, and deposition of relics; that so any unnecessary shock to the feelings of the natives might be avoided, and they might be the more ready to worship the true God, if they could do so in their accustomed fanes. Further, their old sacrificial feasts are only to be changed in character, not abolished. On the days of the dedication of their temples as churches, and on the festivals of the saints whose relics had been placed in them, the people are to erect booths of branches round the buildings, and there feast on the animals they had formerly sacrificed to demons, keeping solemn festival, and giving thanks to the Creator. "For," the letter proceeds, "it is obviously impossible to cut off everything at once from hard minds; since he who would reach the top of a hill must ascend step by step, not by jumps. So the Lord, when he made Himself known to the Israelites in Egypt, reserved to His own worship the same sacrifices as they had been used to offer to devils: the same animals were retained, yet the sacrifices were not the same, being thenceforth offered to God."[1]

The messengers, Laurentius and the monk Peter, who returned from Rome with the aforesaid replies to Augustine, carried also letters to Queen Bertha and King Ethelbert. To this effect Gregory wrote to the queen: "We have been informed what kindness and charity your Glory has displayed towards our most

[1] B. IX., Ind. iv., Ep. 71.

reverend brother and fellow-bishop Augustine, and how God has graciously granted the conversion of the English nation as your reward. You have been to the English what Helena, the mother of Constantine, was to the Romans. But you ought already to have brought your influence further to bear on our glorious son your consort, so that through him the conversion of the whole English nation may be brought about. With your sound faith and literary accomplishments you ought to find this task neither slow nor difficult. Delay not then to strengthen your glorious husband's love of the gospel by continual exhortation, and inflame his zeal for a complete conversion of the whole nation. So may the good things spoken of you be found in all respects true, and increase. You are already known and prayed for at Rome, nay your fame has reached Constantinople and even the ears of the most serene emperor: your Christianity already fills us on the earth with joy: so strive that for your perfected work there may be joy among the angels in heaven." The following is the purport of the letter to the king :—

"For this end does the Almighty exalt good men to rule over nations, that through them He may bestow the gifts of His grace on their subjects. Take this view of your position, my glorious son; hasten to spread the Christian faith in your dominions: put down idolatry, overthrow heathen buildings; by exhortations, terrors, blandishments, corrections, and example, build up your people in great purity of life. So may He whose kingdom you shall have extended on earth reward you in heaven, and make your name glorious to posterity. You have with you Augustine the bishop, thoroughly instructed in monastic rule, full of sacred knowledge, and abounding in good works. Listen to his admonitions, remember them, and act upon them. So will God the more readily hear his prayers in your behalf. For how could God hear him for you, should you refuse (which God forbid) to hear him for God? Throw yourself therefore into the fervour of his zeal, and support him in all his efforts. Further we would have your Glory know that we learn from the Lord's own words in Hóly Scripture that the end of the present world is now at hand, and the eternal reign of the saints about to begin. As the day approaches, there will be extraordinary events;— changes in the air, terrors from heaven, seasons out of natural order, wars, famines, pestilences, earthquakes in divers places. All will not come in our day; all will come soon. Whatever signs of this kind you perceive in your land, regard them as signs of the end, warning us to be solicitous for our souls, and prepared for judgment. I write but shortly of these things now: I will explain them more at length when your nation is more extensively converted; for then I shall be more disposed to write with no reserve. I send you a few small presents in token of friendship, which will not be small to you, since you receive them from me with the blessing of the blessed Apostle Peter. Almighty God preserve and perfect His grace begun in you, and after a long life here, receive you in the congregation of the heavenly country!"[1]

[1] B. IX., Ind. iv., Epp. 59, 60.

These two letters are strikingly illustrative of Gregory's shrewd and delicate diplomacy in addressing potentates; appealing to motives likely to be cogent in each case, and taking care to commend his exhortations by the introduction of gratifying compliments. And indeed his whole recorded action in instituting and controlling the English mission affords a good example, not only of his unceasing zeal for the propagation of the faith, but also of his watchful eye, his mastery of details, his perception of the circumstances to be dealt with, his fine judgment and good sense. The main point in which he failed of his purpose, and in which he has been censured by some, is his design of subjecting the ancient independent British Church to the Roman see, which has been often adduced as an instance of unjustifiable papal aggression. But this design was in accordance with the view he sincerely held of the universal supremacy of St. Peter's chair; and he probably anticipated no such resistance as ensued from the remote and friendless Britons. Nor, considered apart from the question of the legitimacy of the authoritative claim, was the design in itself either unwise or hopeless. It was surely a wise policy to endeavour to amalgamate the old Celtic churches of these islands into the united commonwealth of Western Christendom. Had they remained permanently isolated, under the domination, without appeal, of half-civilized kings and chieftains, it is difficult to imagine for them a prosperous or healthy future. And that the scheme was in itself feasible is shown by the fact that it appears to have been mainly Augustine's impolitic stiffness which prevented its immediate realization with regard to the Britons in Wales, and that it was accomplished in due time, though not in the days of Gregory.

After the above account of Gregory's dealings with the Church among the Franks, and his missionary work in Britain, we may fitly introduce his action in regard to religious matters with his nearer neighbours the Lombards, over whom also he gained influence through correspondence with a Catholic queen. His political relations to this formidable nation have already been noticed; and it has appeared how, through Theodelinda, the wife of King Agilulph, the latter had twice been induced to withdraw for a time from the Roman territory, and conclude a peace. The Lombards, as has been said, were Arians, and spoken of originally as violently prejudiced. But she was a Catholic Christian, being the daughter of Garibald, the Catholic king of Bavaria. It was to her that King Agilulph was indebted for his crown; for she had been the widow of the former king, Antharis, who had died without issue, and whose subjects had decided upon accepting as king the second husband whom she might choose. She selected Agilulph, duke of Turin, who thus became king of the Lombards.[1] Thus the circumstances of her position would be likely to give her influence over her Arian husband, while the confidence placed in her after the former king's death implies that she was one whose character commanded esteem. We may be sure, from what we have seen of Gregory, that he would not let

[1] Paul. Diacon.

slip such an opportunity of obtaining a footing for the true faith; and accordingly we find him keeping up a correspondence with her in his affectionate and courtly style, and urging her to influence the king. In a letter, for instance, of thanks and congratulation addressed to her on the conclusion of peace through her influence in 599, he adds the following admonition: "Saluting you with paternal love, we exhort you so to deal with your most excellent consort that he may not reject the society of the Christian republic. For, as we believe you also know, it will be in many ways useful, if he should be willing to embrace its friendship. Do you, therefore, after your manner, be zealous for whatever tends to the reconciliation of parties, and, wherever there is a prospect of reward, labour to commend your good works more fully before the eyes of Almighty God." He wrote on the same occasion to Agilulph himself, thanking him for the peace concluded, and requesting him to provide for its continuance; but, with characteristic tact, avoids allusion to the delicate subject touched on in his communication to the queen.[1] It is about this date (599) that the king's conversion to Catholicity, followed by that of a great part of his subjects, is believed to have been at length effected through the influence of Theodelinda, which is said to have brought about a general rebuilding of churches and monasteries which had been destroyed in the Lombard ravages, and the restoration of banished Catholic bishops to their sees. After this, we do not read of

---

[1] B. VII., Ind. ii., Epp. 41, 42.

any more hostile invasions during the reign of Gregory. And thus we have one more instance of the wisdom of his appreciation of the power of female piety or zeal, and of his policy in cultivating and utilizing the influence of queens. Three queens, Clotilda, Bertha, and Theodelinda, are especially memorable in history as having been the instruments of the conversion of kingdoms, the unbelieving or misbelieving husbands being won by the conversation of the wives, and two of them were moved and inflenced by St. Gregory.

CHAPTER VI.

Accession of Phocas—His Character—His treatment of Mauricius and the Imperial family—Gregory's letters to him—To Leontia—Consideration of Gregory's conduct on this occasion—Its result—Former letters in praise of Mauricius—Palliations—Suffering from gout—Last letter to Theodelinda—Death and burial—Conduct of the mob after his death—Archdeacon Peter—Personal appearance of Gregory—His costume—Ecclesiastical vestments in his day—Relics of him preserved at Rome—(601–606).

In the November of the year 601 a political change took place at Constantinople, in connection with which Gregory appears in a less favourable light than during any other part of his career. Seditions in the army, which was now an important power in the state, aggravated by vacillating attempts of the Emperor Mauricius to enforce discipline, led to the elevation of Phocas, who was but a common centurion, but a favourite with the soldiery stationed on the Danube. Against this upstart the reigning emperor found no sufficient support among his subjects in Constantinople. It is a sign of the degraded state of things in the imperial city, that the two influential parties there, on whom the emperors depended, were those into which the partisans of the games of the circus were divided; designated from the colours which they wore as the Blues and the Greens. Neither Blues nor Greens proving an efficient support, Mauricius had to succumb to his ignoble rival, and, endeavouring with his wife and children to escape to the Asiatic shore, was compelled by opposing winds to take refuge in a church near Chalcedon. Phocas entered Constantinople, was accepted as emperor, and anointed, with his wife Leontia, by Cyriacus, the patriarch. He is represented by all the historians of the period in very black colours; as illiterate, sensual, passionate, and cruel. His very personal appearance—his diminutive and deformed stature, his close shaggy eyebrows, his red hair, his beardless chin, his cheek disfigured by a scar, which grew black when he was in a rage—is spoken of as a fit emblem of his low and savage character. His acts after his accession were in accordance with the picture: five sons of the deposed emperor (the eldest, Theodosius, had been sent to solicit aid from Persia) were murdered in succession before their father's eyes, and then the Emperor himself; their bodies were thrown into the sea, their heads exposed at Constantinople till putrefaction began, and then buried. On witnessing the death of each of his sons, the old father, who was not devoid of piety, is said to have exclaimed, "Thou art just, O Lord, and Thy judgments are right," and to have prevented the pious fraud of a nurse who would have substituted her own infant for one of his. Afterwards the eldest son, Theodosius (who had been associated with his father in the empire when only four years old) was intercepted in his flight to Persia, and beheaded at Nice. The Empress Constantina and her three daughters, who had taken refuge in the church of St. Sophia at Constantinople, where the Patriarch had pledged his oath for their safety, were dragged from sanctuary, on the discovery of a conspiracy in their favour, and beheaded, the Empress having been previously tortured. A host of meaner victims are recorded to have been executed with savage cruelty; scourged to death, their eyes pierced, their hands and feet amputated, their tongues torn out. Leontia, the tyrant's wife, is described as a worthy match for such a husband.[1]

Now it does not follow that Gregory was cognizant of all the atrocities above described, or of the character of the usurper and his wife, when he hailed their elevation in the terms to be now alluded to. But, being usually so well informed of what was going on in various parts of the world, he must, we conceive, have known something of what Phocas was, and at any rate of his treatment of the old emperor and his sons; and, in any case, his exultation on the death of Mauricius, whose fate called for so much sympathy, and the way in which he vilifies him whom he had so lately honoured, cannot but leave on our minds a painful impression of unseemliness.

The new emperor sent, according to custom, images of himself and of his consort to Rome, which, together with the news of his accession, were received by the populace with acclamations of joy. Mauricius had become unpopular there, owing, it may be supposed, to his provoking conduct, and the exactions of his officers, in connection with the Lombard invasions.

---

[1] See Cedrenus, *in Ann. iv. Pho:.*

Gregory wrote thus to Phocas: "Glory to God in the highest, who, according as it is written, changes times and transfers kingdoms. In the incomprehensible dispensation of Almighty God there are vicissitudes in human life; and sometimes, when the sins of many are to be visited, one is raised up through whose hardness the necks of his subjects may be depressed under the yoke of tribulation; as we have experienced in our prolonged affliction. But sometimes, when the merciful God is pleased to refresh the hearts of many mourners, He advances one to supreme power, through the bowels of whose compassion He pours the grace of His exultation into the minds of all; in which abundance of exultation we believe that we shall be speedily confirmed, while we rejoice that the Benignity of your Piety has been raised to the imperial throne. Let the heavens rejoice, and the earth be glad! and may the people of the whole republic, grievously afflicted hitherto, grow cheerful on account of your benignant acts." After this exaggerated preface, Phocas is exhorted to fulfil such glowing hopes by the justice and moderation of his rule; and among other excellent maxims he is reminded of one, which, however good in theory, was not always, it is to be feared, consistent with fact;—that "there is this difference between the kings of the nations and the emperors of the republic, that the former are lords of slaves, but the latter lords of free men."

Again, the new emperor having complained that there was no representative of the Pope at his court according to ancient custom, Gregory wrote saying, "We are pleased to think, with joy and great thanksgiving, what praises we owe to Almighty God, that, the yoke of sadness removed, we have arrived at times of liberty under the imperial piety of your Benignity. For, as to your Serenity not finding a deacon of the Apostolic See according to ancient custom at your court, this is due, not to our negligence, but the most grave necessity. For during the late hard times all the ministers of this our church were afraid to reside in the imperial palace, and we could not impose on any of them the perilous office. But since they have learnt how, through the grace of God, your Clemency has ascended the throne, they, who feared before, are in haste to approach you under the persuasion of joy." The letter concludes,— "How, for the length of thirty years, we have been oppressed by invasions of the Lombards, and perils daily around us, no words can express. But we trust in Almighty God, who will perfect the consolation which He has begun; and, having raised up pious lords over the republic, will also extinguish our cruel enemies. Therefore may the Holy Trinity preserve your life through many years, that we may long enjoy the blessings of your piety which we have tardily received." He wrote also to the Empress Leontia. From what we have seen of Gregory, we might have been sure beforehand that he would not neglect to do this. It is illustrative also of his diplomatic tact, that to her, and not to the Emperor, he broaches the subject which was doubtless prominent in his mind while he thus hailed and adulated the rising suns, —viz., the claims of St. Peter's see; with especial

reference, we may suppose, to his long struggle under
Mauricius against the counter-claims of Constantinople. And, in the hope of securing her interest, he
bids her, in a tone he had not ventured on with the
Emperor, regard the good of her own soul, appealing
to the religious motives which, in this as in other
cases, he counted on especially in the female mind.
He addresses her thus:—"What tongue can speak,
what mind can conceive, the thanks we owe to Almighty God for the serenity of your empire, in that,
the hard burden so long borne having been removed
from our necks, the light yoke has ensued which
subjects delight to bear? Glory, therefore, be given
to the Creator of all by the hymning choirs of heaven,
thanks be rendered by men upon earth; since the
whole republic, which has endured many wounds of
woe, has found the balm of your consolation!" After
praying that the new rulers may combine justice and
gentleness with zeal for the Catholic faith, and that
she especially may imitate the Empress Pulcheria,
who had been called a second Helena, he proceeds:
"Perhaps I ought to have especially commended to
your Tranquillity the Church of the blessed Apostle
Peter, which has up to this time suffered from
grievous hostile schemes; but because I know you
love God, I ought not to ask for what of your own
accord, and out of the benignity of your piety, you
are ready to accomplish. For by how much the
more you love the Creator by so much will you the
more love the Church of him to whom it was said,
'Thou art Peter; and upon this rock will I build My
church, and the gates of hell shall not prevail against

it'; and again: 'To thee will I give the keys of the kingdom of heaven; and whatsoever thou shalt bind on earth shall be bound in heaven; and whatsoever thou shalt loose on earth shall be loosed in heaven.' Whence we doubt not with what strong love you bind yourself to Him through whom you desire to be loosed from the bonds of all your sins. May He, then, be the guardian of your empire, your protector on earth, your intercessor in heaven."[1]

These addresses to Phocas and Leontia leave, as has been said, a painful impression. They constitute the main blot on the character of Gregory. Their fulsomeness may, indeed, be in some degree excused by the exaggerated style in which it was the custom to address imperial personages; and perhaps by a view, entertained on principle, of the deference due to the powers ordained of God, whom it was always the habit of Gregory to treat with great respect. And, as has been also intimated, he may not have been aware at the time how utterly unworthy of such praises these new rulers were. Further, the excessive flattery may be accounted for, though not on this plea excused, by his earnest desire to gain their support in his pending dispute with the Patriarch, which he regarded on principle as being of such great importance. This motive plainly appears in his letter to Leontia. And if this was his main object, the event proved, at any rate, his sagacity. The statement indeed made by Baronius, and since continually repeated, that Phocas formally conferred on

---

[1] B. IX., Ind. vi., Epp. 32, 45, 46.

Pope Boniface III. the title of "Universal Bishop," which had been claimed by the Patriarch, is open to dispute. The old authorities do not say as much as this; and it seems most unlikely that a pope would accept a title which his great predecessor had only a few years before so strongly repudiated for himself. But it is undoubted that the new Emperor took the Pope's part against the Patriarch Cyriacus, the latter having offended him by his protection of Constantina and her daughter, as the former had conciliated him by his flattering support; and that Boniface, who had been Gregory's representative (*apocrisiarius*) at the Constantinopolitan court, having become pope, an imperial decree was issued in favour of the claims of Rome. The words of Anastasius, the biographer of the popes, with reference to this decree, are, "He (*i. e.* Boniface) obtained from the Emperor Phocas that the Apostolic See of St. Peter, that is, the Roman Church, should be the head of all churches, because the Church of Constantinople wrote itself the first of all churches." Whatever might be the effect of this decree (the importance of which has probably been overrated), it was at any rate originally due to Gregory's attitude towards Phocas at the time of his accession. As to his vilification of the deceased Mauricius in the letters above quoted, we may suppose it also mainly due to Gregory's deeply felt grievance with respect to the disputed title, though it is to be remembered that, in connection also with the Lombard invasions, he had long had just cause of great complaint. Still, under the affecting circumstances, the language used was unseemly, especially as Mauricius appears to have been on the whole a fairly good emperor, not without his virtues, and as Gregory had once been accustomed to address him in language such as this :—" Since a sincere rectitude of faith shines in you, most Christian of princes, like a light sent from heaven, and since it is known to all that your Serenity embraces with all your heart the pure profession which wins the favour of God, &c."[1] Again, in acknowledgment of money sent by the Emperor for the relief of distress at Rome :—" The accustomed piety of my lord has so shone forth in this kind relief, that the want of all the distressed has been succoured by the consolation of its liberality. Wherefore we all address our tearful prayers to the Almighty, who has thus moved the heart of your Clemency, that He would preserve the empire of our lords by the constancy of His love. All alike pray with one accord that God may grant you a long and quiet reign, and that your most happy issue may long flourish in the Roman republic."[1] This last communication is assigned, in the Benedictine arrangement of St. Gregory's epistles, to the year 600; and, if this late date be right, the contrast between its tone and that of the letters to Phocas is the more glaring. In any case it is evident that the growing dissatisfaction with the conduct of the Emperor,—apparent already, however veiled by courteous deference, in the letters about the Lombard troubles and the disputed title,— found a sudden vent, in language strangely inconsistent with some previous professions, at the very

---

[1] B. VIII., Ind. iii., Ep. 2.

time when it was expedient to court the usurping rival, and when generosity, or even decency, might have suggested silence.

Gregory's language on this occasion has been dwelt on at some length, as being the one great charge brought against his moral rectitude, which admirers of the splendour of his general character cannot but be anxious to palliate. After all palliations, it remains against him; but the very fact that there is only one such charge of importance is a telling one in favour of any human being; and, after all, it is not perhaps so serious a charge as has been often represented, when we remember that excessive adulation was then the conventional style of addressing emperors and empresses, without which it might be difficult to get their ear at all;—that Gregory's aims throughout were not selfish or wordly, but the advancement of what he sincerely believed to be the cause of God; and (we may add as to his reflections on Mauricius and his exultation at his overthrow) that not only had he been much provoked, but also that he had long been a martyr to gout when he wrote, a circumstance that may excuse much soreness and irritability.

It may be here remarked, with reference to his frequent and prolonged suffering from this disease, that it enhances our admiration of his unwearied activity. He wrote in the year 600 to Eulogius of Alexandria:—" In the last year I received your letter, but have been unable to answer it till now, owing to the excess of my illness. For nearly two years I have been confined to my bed, and afflicted with such pains from gout that I have hardly been able to rise for three hours' space on festivals to celebrate mass. I am soon compelled by excess of pain to lie down again, and seek relief by groaning. My pain is sometimes alleviated, and sometimes intense; but never so alleviated as to leave me, nor ever to intense as to kill me. Hence I am daily dying, but never die."[1]

We find him again suffering from the same chronic malady when, in 604, shortly before his death, he addressed his last letter to Theodelinda, the Lombard queen. She had sent to request him to answer a book that had been written by an abbat Secundinus against the condemnation of the three chapters. She had also informed him of the birth of her son Adaloaldus, and his baptism into the Catholic Church. On the latter event he, of course, congratulates her in his usual complimentary style, with prayers for the prosperity and growth in grace of the infant prince; but he regrets that he cannot write an immediate answer to the book because of a severe attack of gout:—"Not only," he says, "are we unable to dictate, we cannot even rise to speak; as your messengers know, who found us weak when they came, and have left us in the utmost danger." He promises, however, a full answer should he recover, and in the mean time sends her the decrees of the fifth council, held under Justinian, in which the three chapters had been condemned, and strongly disclaims the imputation, that the acceptance of these decrees by the popes was open to any suspicion of heresy. Further, he sends for the infant a cross containing wood of the

---

[1] B. VII., Ind. iii., Ep. 35.

true one, and a passage of the Gospels in a Persian case, to be worn as phylacteries; and for his sister three rings, two with hyacinths, and one with a white stone; and, lastly, he sends greetings to the king, with thanks to him for the peace that had been concluded, and entreats the queen to use her accustomed endeavours to keep him in the same mind. With this characteristic letter, which shows no failure in the writer's mental activity, we may close our account of the career of Gregory; adding only that in this last year of his life his letters on matters of business, discipline, charity, and other subjects, were as frequent and as forcible as in any previous period. He did not recover from his illness, but died on the 12th of March in the same year (A.D. 604), and was buried in St. Peter's Church, in which his tomb is now to be seen under the altar of St. Andrew, to whom his monastery at Rome was dedicated.

What occurred in Rome immediately after his death is an example of the fickleness of crowds. The distress that had so long prevailed, and which Gregory had taken such pains to alleviate, had now reached its height, and a general famine had ensued. Thereupon he, the deceased pope, who had been at first hailed by all classes as their only hope, who had been throughout his reign in so many ways the guardian and benefactor of the city, who had collected and expended so much in charity while he had spent so little on himself,—was accused by the populace of having caused the famine by his lavish expenditure. They are said to have been on the point of avenging themselves by destroying his library, had not the Archdeacon Peter stayed their fury by asserting that he had seen the Holy Ghost in the form of a dove hovering above his head as he wrote his books. Peter died suddenly in the pulpit as he was about to confirm this statement with an oath; and this was curiously enough taken as a confirmation of its truth; and so the library was spared.[1] Hence it is that St. Gregory is represented in art with a dove above his head.

We all feel a natural desire to form an idea of the personal appearance of distinguished men who have long passed away from earth. We are enabled to do this in the case of Gregory, as far as words can present a picture, from the description by John the Deacon, his biographer, of a portrait of the saint in his monastery of St. Andrew, supposed to have been placed there by himself, and extant in the writer's time, which was the 9th century. John concludes that Gregory himself had it painted during life, from an inscription appended to it, which implies this, and from the head being surmounted, not by a "corona," but by a "tablet" (*tabula*), which is said to denote a person still alive. The portraits of his father and mother placed by Gregory in the same monastery have been described above, and it has been mentioned how his own features combined the characteristics of both. His figure is further described as of ordinary height, and well-made; the beard as somewhat tawny and of moderate length; round his large and round bald crown he has dark

---

[1] Life by John the Deacon, iv. 69.

hair, decently curled and hanging under the ears; on his high forehead are two neat little curls twisting towards the right; the eyebrows are long, slender, and elevated; the pupils not large, but open, and of a yellow tinge, and the lower eyelids full; the nose is thin as it descends from the eyebrows, broader about the middle, slightly aquiline, and expanded at the nostrils; the cheeks are regular; the lips ruddy, thick, and subdivided; the chin rather prominent from the confines of the jaws; the expression of countenance is mild. There is a little uncertainty as to the meaning of the words used in describing the complexion. They probably mean that it was swarthy and fresh, free from the unhealthy hue which it acquired before the end of life. It is added that his hands are well-formed, the fingers taper, and well adapted for writing. His dress is a chestnut-coloured "planeta" over a "dalmatic." Now, though these articles of dress have long been confined to the officiating clergy, the former being, in fact, the eucharistic "chasuble," yet it is undoubted that, like other ecclesiastical vestments, they were originally parts of ordinary costume, worn by the laity as well as the clergy. The dalmatic was a long tunic with sleeves, the planeta an upper garment, in the form, it is said, of a circle, with a hole in the middle through which the head was passed. And it is confirmatory of the view that they had no sacred significance in the time of Gregory, that his father is described as wearing in his portrait precisely the same dress, and of the same chestnut colour. It does not, however, follow that they wore at that time the costume of every-day life, since the dalmatic, at least, seems to have been retained as a tunic of ceremony for state officials, as well as for ecclesiastics, after it had passed out of ordinary use. It is still part of the coronation robes of kings both in England and elsewhere; and Gordianus may have worn both it and the planeta in his capacity of "Regionarius."[1] But the Pope himself is distinguished from his father by wearing also a "pallium" or "pall," marking his ecclesiastical position. When he sent this ensign of jurisdiction to metropolitans, we find him usually directing that they were to wear it only during the celebration of mass. We may conclude, perhaps, from such directions, and from his being painted with it on, that his own supreme jurisdiction was marked by his wearing it ordinarily, or, at any rate, when he pleased. This, however, does not necessarily follow, since the portrait represents him as having a book of the Gospels in one hand, and making the sign of the cross with the other, which attitude may be meant to signify his being engaged in some sacred function, and giving a benediction. If so, it would appear that, but for the pallium, he officiated in a dress that was also worn by laymen. The form of the pallium, and the mode of wearing it at that time, is further denoted by the description of the portrait, and by another, given also by John the Deacon, of one of Gregory's own palls, which had been preserved to the writer's day. It seems to have been

---

[1] *See* Wharton Marriot's "*Vestiarium Christianum.*"

simply a long narrow strip of white linen, unembroidered, worn with its middle part hanging loose over the breast, passing over the left shoulder and behind the neck; crossed over the right, and with its two ends hanging down, at the back and at the side.

The biographer speaks also of other relics of the saint still preserved, and venerated on his anniversary; viz., his "phylactery" (or case for relics or amulets) of thin silver, with a bit of common cloth for hanging it round the neck; and his belt, only a thumb's breadth in width. He speaks of all these as denoting the monastic simplicity of Gregory's habits. He mentions elsewhere, as preserved in the song-school at Rome, which Gregory had built, his original Antiphonary (or book of Antiphons), the couch on which he used to recline, and the whip with which he menaced the boys when he taught them singing. Here we have, by the way, a further evidence of his personal superintendence of everything. He seems to have done nothing by deputy that he could do himself. And the mention of the couch is interesting as implying how he persevered even in this humble duty when he was too ill to sit up.

CHAPTER VII.

Gregory's writings—His letters—Extracts from them—To the Subdeacon Peter—To Marinianus of Ravenna—To Dominicus of Centumcellæ—To Maximus of Salona—To the Ex-prefect Libertinus—To Gregoria, a lady at court—To the Emperor's sister, Theoctista—Another letter to the same lady—Liber Pastoralis Curæ—Its renown—Its plan—Summary of its contents—The Book of Dialogues—Occasion of its composition—Its contents—References to Benedict of Nursia—The fourth book about the state of the soul after death—Its effects on Christian thought—Commentary on Job—Milman's account of it—Specimens of its style—Homilies—On Ezekiel—On the Gospels—Extracts—Sacramentary, Antiphonary, Hymns—The Lord's Prayer in the Eucharistic Office—Genuineness and style of the Hymns—Gregorian and Ambrosian music.

By his writings, as well by his administration, Gregory left a mark upon his age, and has largely influenced succeeding ones. Some account of his extant works, with a few illustrative extracts, will serve to show the nature of his influence in this way, and to elucidate his own inner mind and character.

First, then, we have his letters, which have been often referred to above, and from which many extracts have been given. The number preserved amounts to 838, many of them being long ones. They are addressed to persons of various ranks and positions in all parts of the world that he had to do with;—to emperors and empresses, kings and queens, patriarchs, bishops, abbats, clergy, legates, and other agents of the Apostolic See, stewards of its estates, ladies, and other private persons. They treat a large range of subjects;—politics, diplomacy, doctrine, ecclesiastical discipline, relations of Church and State, papal claims, missionary work, monasticism, management of property (with especial reference to equitable treatment of tenants and serfs), works of charity, directions to individuals on matters of duty and conscience. Nothing could give us a more striking impression of the writer's grasp of the multifarious duties of his position, his minute personal attention to all, and the versatility of his powers; while they often reveal to us, as only letters can, his character and sentiments.

The following extracts, taken here and there from the collection, in addition to what we have quoted in the course of his life, may help to bring the man more fully before us.

Here we have a long letter to Peter, his subdeacon in Sicily, acting as a general agent in ecclesiastical as well as secular affairs, whom he had sent thither for the purpose as early as 591. It is characteristic of the writer in many ways. In it he says: "I remember to have written desiring you to dispense to certain monasteries, and for other purposes, certain legacies that have been left to me. But for some cause to me unknown you have not done this. I charge you, therefore, to pay the value of these legacies out of the church funds for the purposes designated, lest, when you leave the country, you leave behind you the groans of the poor against you." Again: "I hear that a certain lady left when dying, but by word of mouth only, a silver shell to be sold for the benefit of her freedman, and a silver shield to a monastery. Both bequests, though not legally binding, must be carried out in every particular, lest from the smallest things we incur the greater guilt." Again: "It appears that there are certain things on our farms, which, though you know them to belong to other persons, you have not restored to their rightful owners, yielding to pressure and to fear. But if you were truly a Christian, you would fear the judgment of God more than the voices of men. Attend then to my unceasing admonitions on the subject." Further: "In the case of the son of Scholasticus, you inform me that he demands more than is legally just. But as we are unwilling to be hard upon the poor, and as he has had much trouble in the matter, we desire you to give him 50 *solidi*, aud to charge this sum in your accounts." Again: We have learnt that Sisinnius, who was a judge at Samnium, is now in Sicily in great want. We desire you to allow him 20 casks of wine and 4 *solidi* yearly." Then follow other directions to give donations to individuals known to be in need. In other parts of the same letter he treats a different class of subjects, therein showing peculiar kindliness. He says, for instance, "You must know that some time ago I conceived a strong dislike to the servant of God Pretiosus, for no great fault, and repelled him from my presence sad and embittered. For this I have since been very sorry. I wrote to ask the lord bishop to send him to me, but he is unwilling to part with him. But I hear that Pretiosus himself is in distress at not being allowed to come. Hence I am in doubt what to do, since I must not and cannot distress the bishop, who, occupied as he is with the affairs of God, ought to be supported by comfort, not saddened by bitterness. Wherefore, if your wisdom is greater than that little body which contains it, manage it so that I may have my will without distressing the lord bishop. But if you perceive that he takes the matter at all to heart, say no more about it." Further on,—"I have been very sorry to hear that the lord bishop has excommunicated Eusebius, a man of such advanced age, and in such bad health. Wherefore it is needful that you admonish the bishop privately not to be precipitate in passing sentences." Here tenderness in the exercise of discipline is recommended; in another case strictness seems to be insisted on: "Presume not to say anything about Gelasius, the subdeacon, since his crime is such as to demand the heaviest penance to the end of his life." After this sharp admonition, our Pope, who, to his credit, had a sense of humour, passes at once into a vein of pleasantry. Little Peter, though he seems to have wanted looking after sometimes, was not so bad but that the Pope could enjoy a pleasant joke against him. "Besides" (the letter continues, and this "besides" comes close after the sharp admonition, in the same breath as it were; suggesting the idea that the preceding sentence might be also a pleasantry), "Besides, you have sent me one wretched horse and five good asses. The horse I cannot ride, he is such a bad one; the good beasts I cannot ride, because they are asses. But if you wish to keep me your friend, pray let me have something worthy of you."[1]

As a specimen of his kindly consideration for others, and of humanity and good sense modifying his ascetic strictness, may be quoted three successive letters written in 601 to Marinianus, bishop of Ravenna, his old friend in St. Andrew's, with whom, on his first promotion, he had had a dispute (as has been mentioned) about the use of the pallium. They are the more significant of his kindly thoughtfulness from having been written while he was himself suffering from one of his agonizing attacks of gout. He says, "For a long time I have been unable to rise from my bed. I am tormented by the pains of gout; a kind of fire seems to pervade my whole body: to live is pain; and I look forward to death as the only remedy." .... "Great has been my sorrow to hear of your Fraternity suffering from vomiting of blood. With regard to which affection I have anxiously caused the most learned medical men here to be separately consulted, and I send to your holiness in writing what they severally think and recommend. Above all things, they advise quiet and silence, which I greatly doubt whether you can have in your church. And therefore it seems to me that, provision having been made for its episcopal supervision, for the celebration of masses, for the exercise of hospitality, and for the superintendence of monasteries, you ought to come to me before the summer season, that I may personally, as far as I

---

[1] B. II., Ind. x., Ep. 32.

can, provide for your sickness, and guard you from disturbance; since the physicians say that the summer time is peculiarly unfavourable to your complaint. And I greatly fear lest, if you have any cares in addition to the adverse season, you may be in danger of a relapse. I myself, also, am exceedingly weak, and it is altogether desirable that you should, through the favour of God, return in health to your church; or certainly, if you are to be called away, that you should be called in the hands of your friends. And I too, who see myself to be near death, if it shall please God to call me before you, would wish to pass away in your hands. If, therefore, you feel yourself still suffering from the same complaint, and arrange to come, you need bring but few attendants with you, since you will live with me, and in this church you will have daily attendance. Further, I neither exhort nor admonish you, but I strictly order you, that you by no means presume to fast, since the physicians say that abstinence is very bad for your complaint. Only, if some great solemnity requires it, I allow you to fast on five occasions during the year. . . . . This I say in order that, if you should feel yourself better and should delay your visit, you may know what my command requires you to observe."[1]

The following extracts may serve as specimens of numerous letters providing for the protection of widows or other persons liable to oppression. To Dominicus, Bishop of Centumcellæ (*Civita Vecchia*):

[1] B. XI., Ind. iv., Epp. 32, 33, 40.

"It belongs to the priestly office to impart consolation to widows; so that, deprived in this world of human protection, they may find a remedy in the Church's guardianship. Since then, Luminosa, an honourable lady, relict of the beloved tribune Zemarchus, has committed herself to our protection after that of God, we admonish you to give her solace in all things needful, and allow no one to be in any way troublesome to her. So may you have God for your debtor, and so may our mind more heartily thank you for the consolations you have afforded."[1]

To Maximus, Bishop of Salona, who had complained of an invasion of the Sclaves, and also of the injustice of an unjust judge in his province, Gregory writes a letter, in which his pious sentiments and the prudence of his counsel, as well as his accustomed care for the oppressed, are conspicuous:—"Concerning Julianus (the unjust judge), of whom you write, I know not what to say; since I see how everywhere for our sins we are perturbed by enemies from without and by unjust judges among ourselves. But be not altogether cast down by such things; for those who shall come after us will see worse times still, and esteem our days happy in comparison with their own. You are bound, as far as you possibly can, to offer yourself as a champion of the poor and oppressed. If you can do but little good, the devotion of the heart satisfies God who gave it. Omit nothing which may please Him. For human terrrors and favours are like smoke which a light breeze carries away.

[1] B. I., Ind. ix., Ep. 13.

And be assured that no one can please both bad men and God. Consider, then, that in proportion as you have displeased bad men you have pleased God. Still let your defence of the poor be moderate and grave; lest if you proceed at all too sharply, men should think you actuated by youthful pride. Your defence of the oppressed should be such that the humble may feel protection, but the oppressors may not easily find anything for their malevolence to find fault with. Remember what Ezekiel says, 'Son of man, the unbelieving and rebellious are with thee, and thou dost dwell among scorpions'; and the blessed Job, 'I am a brother of dragons and a companion of owls.'"[1] The following letter to Libertinus, an ex-prefect who had become involved in calamity, is an instance both of fatherly exhortation and of delicate benevolence: "From what distresses of this present world you are suffering is not unknown to us. But, since to those who are in the utmost tribulation the only consolation is the mercy of God, rest all your hope on Him, and turn to Him with all your heart, who with justice allows whom He will to be afflicted, and mercifully delivers those that trust in Him. To Him, therefore, give thanks, and bear patiently whatever may be laid upon you. For it is the part of a right mind not only to bless God in prosperity, but also to praise Him in adversity. In the midst, then, of your present sufferings let no murmur against God creep into your heart, since the purpose of our Creator is unknown to us. For perchance, my

---

[1] B. X., Ind. iii., Ep. 36.

illustrious son, you committed some offence against Him when you were placed in prosperity, from which He would purge you by merciful bitterness. And so let neither temporal affliction break you down nor the loss of wealth torment you, since if by thanksgiving and patience in adversity you win God's favour, then both far more than you lost is restored to you, and in addition eternal joys are secured. Now I pray you not to take it amiss that I have ordered twenty suits of clothing to be supplied through Romanus, the defensor, for your servants. For, though it is but a small offering, yet, coming from the property of St. Peter, it is to be taken as representing a great blessing; since he will be able to give you much greater things, even eternal benefits with Almighty God."[1]

The next letter that shall be quoted (and it is worth quoting at some length) exhibits Gregory to us as the spiritual adviser of a lady of rank. It is to Gregoria, a lady of the bedchamber to the empress Constantina, who had opened her conscience to him. "I have received the welcome letter of your sweetness, in which you have been careful to accuse yourself of a multitude of sins. But I know that you fervently love God, and I trust in His mercy, that of you, as once of a certain holy woman, the sentence already proceeds from the mouth of Truth, 'Her sins which are many are forgiven; for she loved much.' But how they were forgiven to that holy woman is shown by this; that she afterwards sat at the Lord's feet, and heard the Word from His mouth. For, taken up

---

[1] B. X., Ind. iii., Ep. 31.

by the contemplative life, she had already transcended the active life which her sister Martha still pursued. She sought also the Lord when buried, and, bending anxiously over the tomb, found not His body. But, when the disciples had gone away, she stood weeping at the entrance of the sepulchre, and Him whom she sought as dead she was accounted worthy to see alive, and announced to the disciples that the Lord was risen. She saw Him, she approached Him, she touched His feet. Bring before your eyes, I pray you, what hand touched whose feet. That woman who had been a sinner in the city, those hands that had been polluted with iniquity, touched His feet who sits at the right hand of the Father, exalted above the angels. Let us conceive, if we can, the bowels of supernal compassion, that a woman who had been sunk in the depth of the gulf through sin was raised aloft on the wing of love through grace. It is fulfilled, most sweet daughter, it is fulfilled, that what at the present church season is being announced to us in the voice of prophecy; 'In that day the house of David shall be an open fountain for the washing away of sin and of uncleanness.' . . . But, as to what your sweetness has added in your letter, that you importunately wait for my writing to you to say that it has been revealed to me that your sins are forgiven;—you ask for what is both difficult and useless: difficult, because I am unworthy of having a revelation made

---

[1] It will be observed that Gregory, according to the ancient tradition, identifies the woman that had been a sinner, the sister of Martha, and the Magdalene.

to me; useless, because you ought not to feel secure about your sins till in the last hour of your life you shall be unable to bewail them. St. Paul, after he had ascended into the third heaven, and been led into Paradise, and heard secret words such as it was not lawful for man to utter, was still afraid and said, 'I keep under my body, and bring it into subjection, lest by any means, when I have preached to others, I myself should be a castaway.' . . . Consider, most sweet daughter, that security is wont to be the mother of negligence. You ought not therefore to have in this life the security that may make you negligent. For it is written, 'Happy is the man that feareth always': and again, 'Serve the Lord with fear, and rejoice with trembling.' In short it is necessary that in the time of this life trembling keep possession of your mind, that you may exult hereafter for ever in the joy of security."[1]

Another longer epistle to the Emperor's sister, Theoctista, who appears to have been governess to the imperial children, is further illustrative of character and mode of thought, and in many respects interesting. Being a religious lady, she had written to him in a pious strain, sending him at the same time large sums to be expended in charity. He begins his reply, "That your Excellency, though placed in such a tumult of affairs, is full of the fruitfulness of the sacred Word, and sighs incessantly for eternal joys, I give great thanks to Almighty God; in that in you I see fulfilled what was written of the elect

[1] B. VII., Ind. xv., Ep. 25.

fathers, 'The children of Israel walked on dry land through the midst of the sea.'" After more of similar purport he goes on, "But in your Excellency's letter I find this deficiency; that you have been unwilling to indicate to me concerning the most serene empress, whether she reads diligently, and with what kind of compunction she is affected when she reads. For your presence ought to profit her much; so that among the waves of affairs under which she continually suffers, and by which, whether she will or not, she is dragged abroad, she may ever be recalled inwardly to the love of her heavenly country: and this also you ought to investigate, as often as tears are granted her for the state of her soul, whether her compunction still comes of fear, or now at last of love." A lengthy explanation follows of the distinction between two kinds of compunction, both of which may find vent in tears, but one of which is due only to the fear of punishment, the other, into which the first ought to grow, to the love of God possessing the thirsty soul. And in a very characteristic strain, he adduces the story of Achsah,[1] in the book of Joshua, as typifying the experience of a soul. Her sitting upon an ass denotes the soul having already overcome the irrational motions of the flesh, and attained to faith and good works: her sighing still, and desiring from her father "springs of water," not content with the dry land of the South that he had given her, denotes the longing

---

[1] Joshua xv. 18, 19. In the Vulgate, which was the translation of the Bible used by St. Gregory, for "she lighted off her ass" of our English version, the rendering is, "she sighed as she sat upon an ass."

of the soul for the grace of tears. But this grace, the grace of compunction, is of two kinds; that of the "nether springs," and that of the "upper springs." The "nether springs" denote compunction arising from the fear of punishment; the "upper springs" denote compunction arising from a love of the heavenly kingdom. It is added that, though the compunction of love comes in fact after the compunction of fear, yet the upper springs are mentioned first in the text because they are of higher dignity than the lower ones. The letter proceeds: "You therefore, who through the operation of Almighty God know by experience both kinds of compunction, ought daily and assiduously to investigate the state of mind of your most serene mistress, and as far as you can by words to profit her. I beg you also to attend carefully to the moral training of the little lords whom you are bringing up, and to admonish the glorious eunuchs who are appointed to attend on them, that they say such things to them as may move them to mutual love, and clemency towards their subjects, lest they now conceive any ill will that may hereafter break out openly. For the words of educators are either milk if they are good, or poison if they are bad." Reference is next made to the large sum of money sent by the pious lady for charitable uses, for which warm thanks are rendered. Some of it had been applied to the redemption of captives taken by the Lombards; the rest to the purchase of bedclothes for the nuns of Rome, who are described as suffering from "grievous nudity" during the severe cold then prevailing. There were as many as 3,000 of them in the city, leading such lives, Gregory says, and so devoted to abstinence and tears, that he believes it to be due to them that any of the inhabitants had escaped the sword of the Lombards. Lastly, he tells the lady that he is sending her a key from the body of St. Peter, that is from his tomb or shrine, which was a present often sent by him to persons likely to appreciate the blessing which it was supposed to convey. And he relates a story of a miracle, so called, that had been wrought through this particular key, which is not a bad sample of one class of incidents then accounted miraculous. It was, it seems, a golden one, and had been once sent to a city of the Lombards, where a certain man had discovered it, and, without regard to its sanctity, was about to cut it with a knife for his own purposes; but, under a divine impulse, he had cut his own throat instead. Antharis, the Lombard king, had been so affected by the supposed miracle that he had sent the key back to Rome with another like it, also of gold, as an offering to the Apostle. The whole of this long letter is rich in illustrations of St. Gregory's mind and character;—of his flattering courtesy to persons of rank, his care for individual souls, his watch especially over the minds and conscience of influential potentates, his analysis of the inner religious life, his style of allegorical exposition of Scripture, his discriminating benevolence, his high appreciation of monastic sanctity, as well as of general female piety; and lastly his superstitious credulity, without the addition of which the picture would be incomplete.

There is another lengthy epistle, written in 601, to

the same lady, which is well worth study. She had been accused by certain persons in Constantinople of holding, with others, erroneous views, and had been much distressed in consequence. Gregory exhorts her at great length to disregard unfounded calumny, satisfied with the testimony of her own conscience; representing to her how trials from evil men are necessary for the probation of the good, and how all the saints of Holy Scripture had been subject to such trials. But, at the same time, he reminds her that, though some sort of calumnies ought to be entirely despised and unnoticed, yet that others ought to be met, in the hope of removing the false impression on which they rest. Of the latter kind were the calumnies against her. She ought, therefore, to summon her principal accusers to a private interview, and disclaim, with an oath if necessary, the views imputed to her. She must not think it unworthy of her, as being of the imperial family, thus to satisfy her inferiors in rank : " For we are all brethren, made by the power, and redeemed by the blood, of one Emperor; and so we ought in no way to look down upon our brethren, however poor and abject." The views which Theoctista was accused of holding were these: 1. That marriages might be dissolved, or married persons live apart from each other, except by mutual consent, under the pretext of religion: 2. That baptism did not convey absolution from all past sins: 3. That three years passed in penitence gave license to sin in future : 4. That an anathema against beliefs imputed to a person was not binding on him, if uttered under compulsion. Against all these positions Gregory argues earnestly, and thus ends his letter: "Wherefore your Excellency, living as you do incessantly in reading, tears, and alms, ought thus to pacify the ignorant by mild exhortations and replies; so as to attain for them as well as for yourself, the glory of eternal reward. My great love for you has induced me thus to speak, since I think that your joy is my gain, and your sadness my loss. May Almighty God guard you by His heavenly grace, and prolong your life for the education of our young lords."[1]

The specimens of his correspondence above given, together with those that have appeared in the preceding narrative, may serve to show how he wrote, and what manner of man he was.

Among his other writings, his "Liber Pastoralis Curæ," a treatise on the responsibilities and duties of the episcopal office, stands pre-eminent for its wide renown. Leander of Seville, to whom he sent it, circulated it in Spain; the emperor Mauricius had it translated into Greek; Alfred the Great himself translated it into English; a succession of synods in Gaul enjoined a knowledge of it on all bishops; and Hincmar, Archbishop of Rheims in the ninth century, says that a copy of it was delivered, together with the book of Canons, to bishops at ordination, with a charge to frame their lives according to its precepts. It deserves its reputation, being a worthy addition to the other two great works of antiquity on the same subject, by S. Chrysostom

[1] B. VII., Ind. xi., Ep. 26; B. XI., Ind. iv., Ep. 45.

and S. Gregory Nazianzen, and more practical than either. The book is addressed to John, Bishop of Ravenna, who had blamed Gregory for his reluctance to accept the popedom, its immediate purpose being to justify such reluctance on the ground of the tremendous responsibility of the pastoral office. It consists of four books, the plan of which is thus explained in the preface:—"The discussion in this treatise is fourfold, that it may approach the mind of the reader in the way of ordered steps. For, as reason requires, it is first to be considered in what manner a man should enter upon the office of government; when he has rightly entered, how he should live; when he lives well, how he should teach; when he teaches aright, how he should know and consider his own infirmity." On the first head, the prevalent practice of hunting after preferment for the sake of power and position, is severely reprobated. Persons, it is said, ignorant of medicine would blush to profess themselves physicians; yet it is common for those who have no knowledge or experience in spiritual things to have no scruple, for the sake of worldly pre-eminence, in professing the deeper and more difficult art of ministering to the diseases of souls. The qualifications which may justify a man in undertaking this arduous office are, first, religious and theological knowledge, to be acquired by study; secondly, a life conformable. He enlarges on this last head. Nothing, he says, does more harm in the Church than the bad example of those whose sacred office commands respect. Besides, he asks, how can those intercede with God for others, who are not themselves at peace with God? And there is, moreover, a peculiar danger to personal holiness in the sacred office, since the variety of cares attending it is apt to divert the pastor from watchfulness over himself. Above all things pride, the besetting temptation of prelates, is to be guarded against; a temptation of peculiar force in the state of things then existing, in which, through God's guidance, religion and its teachers were held in high honour by the great ones of the earth. It is easy and common, he adds, for men to deceive themselves as to their own motives in seeking the pastoral office; purposing to themselves to do great good, while inwardly actuated all the time by a craving for praise and honour; and so, having attained at last what their hearts were really set on, they soon forget their former pious thoughts and resolves. The aspirant, therefore, must be careful to satisfy himself beforehand of the absence from his mind of all such worldly motives; for he will not easily learn humility in a high position, if he has been without it in a low one, or disregard praise when it flatters him, if he has longed for it before it came. On the other hand, it is acknowledged to be the positive duty of such as are fit for it, and do not seek it from worldly motives, to accept the burden of episcopacy. In this connection, one of those curious applications of Scripture is brought in for which Gregory is famous. The brother who, under the law of Moses, was required to espouse the deceased brother's wife, is made to represent pastors, who are bound to marry Christ's spouse the Church, so as to raise up seed to Him. And thus it may be even a sin, and not true humility, to persist in declining office;

"For he is not truly humble who understands it to be the will of God that he should occupy a high position, and yet despises it. But, yielding himself to the divine guidance, and averse from the vice of obstinacy, he ought in his heart to fly from it, and still unwillingly to obey. Nay, there are cases in which persons may laudably desire the office of preaching, while others as laudably may accept it only when forced on them. The prophets Isaiah and Jeremiah are examples. Isaiah, when the Lord asked whom He should send, offered himself of his own accord, saying, 'Here am I, send me.' But Jeremiah is sent, and yet humbly pleads that he should not be sent, saying, 'Ah, Lord God! behold, I cannot speak, for I am a child.' Lo, from these two prophets different voices proceeded outwardly, but they flowed from the same fountain of love. For there are two precepts of charity; love of God, and love of our neighbour. Isaiah, desiring through the active life to benefit his neighbour, craves the office of preaching; Jeremiah, longing, through the contemplative life, to cleave closely to the love of his Maker, remonstrates against being sent to preach. Wherefore what the one laudably desired, the other laudably shrank from. But in both this is to be closely observed, that he who refused did not persist in his refusal, and that he who wished to be sent saw himself to have been already cleansed by a coal from the altar. Hence let no one who has not been cleansed dare to enter upon the sacred ministry; and let no one whom supreme grace has chosen resist proudly under a show of humility."

In the second part, which treats of the duties of

the pastor when he has entered on his office, it is first insisted that he must be pure in thought, and holy in life. "He who by the necessity of his position is required to speak the highest things is compelled by the same necessity to exemplify the highest. For that voice best penetrates the hearts of hearers which the life of the speaker commends, because what he commands in his speech he helps the doing of by his example." Under this head the vestments and ornaments of the High Priest under the Law are adduced with much detail, as typifying the holiness of heart and life required in the Christian bishop. Secondly, he must know when to be silent, and when to speak. "There are many who, for fear of losing the favour of men, are afraid to speak freely what they ought to speak. Such are hirelings, and not shepherds, who, seeing the wolf coming, fly; that is, hide themselves under the veil of silence. . . . . Whosoever enters on the priesthood undertakes the office of a herald, to proclaim with a loud voice the coming of the Judge who follows terribly. Wherefore if the priest knows not how to preach, what loud cry shall the mute herald give? Therefore it was that the Holy Spirit rested on the first pastors under the appearance of tongues; because whomsoever He has filled He causes forthwith to speak. Hence it was that Moses commanded the High Priest to have bells upon him when he went into the sanctuary, as it is written, 'His sound shall be heard when he goeth in unto the holy place before the Lord, and when he cometh out, that he die not.' But, on the other hand, the preacher must be careful

not to speak inopportunely or inordinately: he must not let himself be so hurried into speech as to run the risk of error, or, while perchance he desires to appear wise, unwisely sever the bond of unity. Nay, he ought not only to guard against saying what is amiss, he ought also to avoid saying what is good overmuch and inordinately, since "the incautious importunity of loquacity" lessens the weight of what he says to the heart of the hearers. Thirdly, the good pastor must come close to every one in sympathy, but soar above all in contemplation, "so that through the bowels of compassion he may accommodate himself to the infirmity of others, but through the loftiness of speculation transcend even himself in his aspiration after the invisible; lest either by seeking high things he despise the infirmities of his neighbours, or by suiting himself to the infirmities of his neighbours, he relinquish his desire of high things."
. . . . As Jacob saw the Lord above, and the angels ascending and descending, so good preachers look in contemplation to the Lord, the Head of the Church, above, but descend in sympathy to His members below. Thus Moses went continually in and out of the tabernacle, rapt in contemplation within, occupied with the care of the infirm outside. Thus our Lord continued in prayer on the mountain, but worked miracles in the cities; in this manner showing the way to good pastors, that, while aspiring after the highest, they should mingle in sympathy with the necessities of the infirm; and the more kindly charity descends to the lowest, the more vigorously and wonderfully it recurs to the highest. . . . . The

rulers of the Church should be such that their subjects may not blush to disclose their secrets to them; that the little ones, tost by the waves of temptation, may have recourse to their pastor as to a mother's bosom, and wash away the defilement of the sin that buffets them in the solace of exhortation and the tears of prayer. Fourthly, the pastor must vary his demeanour towards different sorts of people: to those who are living well he must be humble and companionable; against delinquents he must assert his position in his zeal for righteousness; so as in no respect to prefer himself to the good, but fear not to make the perverse feel the power of his pre-eminence. Still, in the latter case, he ought not to rejoice in his power over others, but in his being able to profit them; for our fathers in the faith are spoken of, not as kings of men, but as shepherds of the flock. And in the exercise of discipline he must be tender and considerate; for a fracture is made worse if bound up too tightly: like the good Samaritan, he must pour into the wound both wine and oil; wine to cause smart, but oil for soothing; he must be as a mother in affection, and as a father in discipline; he must be justly compassionate, and affectionately severe; for both justice and mercy fail of their purpose, when one is exercised without the other. Fifthly, the spiritual ruler must be careful neither so to occupy himself with external things as to forget the inner life of the soul, nor so to care for the inner life as to neglect the things which are without. For there are some who give themselves with all their hearts to secular cares, as if they had forgotten that they are set over their brethren for their souls' sake: and so the spiritual life of those who are under them languishes, since, when they desire to advance in it, they find a stumbling-block in the example of their pastor; for, when the head is sick, the members cannot thrive. Others, again, would devote themselves so exclusively to things spiritual as to pay no attention to external affairs, and thus fail entirely to succour the bodily needs of their flock. The preaching of such persons is for the most part despised. For those are not willingly listened to who censure the deeds of delinquents, yet supply them not with the necessaries of this present life. The word of doctrine fails to penetrate the mind of the needy, unless commended by the hand of compassion; but the seed of the word easily germinates when the loving-kindness of the preacher waters it in the hearer's heart. Sixthly, the pastor must guard against anxiety to please men, and caring more for their love than for the truth. For he is an enemy of the Saviour who, through the good works which he does, desires to be loved in the Church instead of God; and it is treason in a servant if, when sent by the Bridegroom with gifts for the Bride, he strives to ingratiate himself with her. Such self-love in the pastor leads both to remissness and to roughness: to remissness, when, for fear of losing the affections of his flock, he "sews pillows to all arm-holes," and flatters when he ought to reprove; to roughness, when, being secure of his position, he constantly inveighs and domineers. It is true that good shepherds should by all means strive to please men; but so as, through love and respect for themselves, to induce them to love the truth; to make the love for themselves to be as a bridge by which the hearts of the hearers may be led to love of the Creator. For it is hard for the preacher, though preaching the truth, to be attended to, if he is not beloved. He should therefore strive to be beloved in order to be heard, but not to seek love for its own sake.

In the third division of the book, which is too long to allow of anything like a complete summary, the subject is, "How the ruler, who lives well, ought to teach and admonish"; detailed distinctions being made between different classes of persons, for whom different kinds of admonition are required. For (it is explained in the preface) the same exhortation does not suit all, as the same herbs do not suit all animals, nor the same medicines all diseases. The intent minds of hearers are like the stretched strings of a harp, each of which the master's hand touches differently, but so as to produce one music. The strings send forth harmony for the very reason that they are all struck by one *plectrum*, but not all with one force. And so every teacher, that he may edify all in the one excellent way of charity, ought to touch the hearts of his hearers out of one doctrine, but not with one and the same exhortation. The following may serve as specimens of the pairs of contrasted characters or positions, of which thirty-six are given, for each of which the fitting style of admonition is pointed out:—Men and women, young and old, poor and rich, the cheerful and the sad, the clever and the stupid, the impudent and the bashful, the impatient and the patient, the healthy and the sick, the silent and the loquacious, the humble and the proud, the gluttonous and the abstinent, the married and the single, the prosperous and the unfortunate, the incontinent and the deliberately wicked, those who are habitually guilty of little sins, and those who, being free from little ones, occasionally fall into great ones, those who do wrong things in secret, but good things in public, and those who hide the good they do, but allow themselves to be thought evil of in their public acts. These and similar contrasted cases are treated at great length, and with much wise discrimination. For instance, with respect to the poor and the rich, the former are to be encouraged and consoled, the latter to be alarmed and warned; but yet with due regard to circumstances, since, in some cases, the poor may be prouder than the rich, or the rich more humble than the poor. Then, as to the silent and the loquacious, the former are to be cautioned lest, in their overstrained fear of improper utterance, they be betrayed into the worse snare of evil cogitations, which may be engendered all the more from the expression of them being suppressed, and from security against discovery; while the loquacious are to be warned how an unbridled tongue diverts a man from self-control and thoughtfulness, and leads him step by step from mere idle talking to slander and uncharitableness. Again, the married are to be admonished not to let their domestic interests interfere with their care for things eternal, but still so that they forget not their duties to each other. They are to be especially urged to mutual consideration and forbearance, the husband thinking not so much of what he has to bear from his wife as what the wife has to bear from him; and the wife likewise. The unmarried, on the other hand, are to take care to be all the more ready for the last day from being free during their probation from earthly cares, and to remember always that it were much better for them to marry than to sin.

Such is the nature of the admonitions under the several heads of the third division of the book.

The fourth and last division, setting forth how "the preacher, having done all things well, should consider himself, lest either his life or his preaching puff him up," is very short, consisting only of a single chapter. In this part it is said, "But since, when an abundant gift of preaching in fitting style is granted, the mind of the speaker is often uplifted by a hidden joy in his own display, great care is necessary, lest while he calls others to salvation he be puffed up so as to neglect his own; lest while he raises others he himself should fall. For to some the very greatness of their excellence has been the occasion of perdition; inordinately secure in their confidence of strength, through negligence they have unexpectedly perished. For excellence struggles with frailties; from a certain delight in it arises flattery of self; and it comes to pass that the mind of one who is doing well throws aside the check of circumspection, and rests secure in self-confidence; and to it in this torpid state the crafty seducer enumerates all its good doings, and exalts it in swelling cogitations, as though surpassing all others. Hence the memory of virtue becomes the pitfall of the soul; since in remembering the good things done, while it raises itself in its own eyes, it falls in the eyes of the Author of Humility." What is said of Israel represents the process: "He delivered their power into captivity, and their beauty into the enemy's hand." David is an example. He said at one time; "In my prosperity I said, I shall never be moved"; but then, again; "Thou didst hide Thy face, and I was troubled." Again; "I have sworn, and I will perform it, that I will keep Thy righteous judgments": but then, again; "I am afflicted very much: quicken me, O Lord, according to Thy word." "Hence it is necessary, when the abundance of our excellences flatters us, that the mind's eye should return to one's infirmity, and lower itself salubriously, so as to see not what has been rightly done, but what has been left undone; that so the heart, being bruised by the recollection of weakness, may be made more robust in excellence before the Author of Humility. And indeed, for this cause God, to whatever extent He perfects the minds of rulers, leaves them usually in some respect imperfect, that, in the midst of the brilliance of their virtues, they may pine for disgust at their imperfection, and by no means exalt themselves for great things, while they are worsted in their strife against the least." In the tone of humility thus enjoined on others, the writer concludes his treatise: "So, good man, compelled by the force of my own reprehension, while I strive to show what a good pastor ought to be, I am like an ill-favoured painter who portrays a handsome man; I direct others to the shore of perfection, while I am myself still tossed among the waves of faults. But in this shipwreck of life, sustain me, I pray, by the plank of thy prayer, that, since my own weight sinks me, thy merit may keep me afloat."

This treatise has been thus summarized at some length on account of both its reputation and its intrinsic value. It contains valuable matter for all times, proceeding evidently from one who had made a careful study of human duty, and of the human heart and conscience, as well as of the art of working on the latter through pastoral influences. It will be observed what essential and prominent parts of a bishop's office preaching and spiritual direction are represented as being. It is these, rather than ceremonial sacerdotal functions, that are the subject of the treatise.

Another work of wide renown is "The Four Books of Dialogues, concerning the Life and Miracles of Italian Fathers and the Eternity of Souls." The writer relates in his preface the occasion of his writing it. He had retired one day to a secret place, oppressed by the cares of office, to brood upon his troubles. The Archdeacon Peter, who had been his close friend from early youth and his companion in study, found him thus musing, and inquired the cause of his deep dejection. He told him in reply how he was constantly harassed by mundane business, which left him no time for heavenly contemplation, how his spiritual state suffered from this cause, and how he continualy looked back with regret to the happy peaceful days he had once spent in his monastery; adding that his sorrow was augmented by the thought of many others, happier than himself, who had renounced the world and attained to great holiness. On Peter replying that he was not aware of Italy having produced any persons so conspicuous for their virtues as to inspire the emulation of Gregory, the latter assures him that if he were to tell him all he knew, either from personal experience or from good testimony, of perfect and approved men, a day would not suffice for the narration. Peter expressing a strong desire to hear what he could tell him, he begins the series of marvellous stories which are the subject of the book, the form of a dialogue being kept up throughout. He acknowledges that he knew them only by hearsay, but undertakes to give his authority in each case, and defends his relating as true what he had not seen himself by the example of St. Mark and St. Luke, who (as, he says, is clearer than the light) record in their Gospels what they had only heard of from others. He premises also that, in some cases, he gives the sense only of what had been told him, not the exact words that had been used, so as to avoid the introduction of rustic speech, unsuitable for a written book.

The stories are mostly of the marvellous order, many of them childish and grotesque; interesting for the view they give us of prevalent beliefs, rather than edifying to readers of the present day. Some of them resolve themselves, on examination, into natural events, to which superstition had given a miraculous colour; some into mental impressions taken for objective realities, or into dreams and trances; others may be due to the exaggeration of vulgar tradition, or to invention only. It is to be observed that Gregory only tells what had been told to him, so that his veracity is not at stake, only his intelligence. It has indeed been often questioned whether a man of his sense and culture could possibly believe such old wives' tales as some of the stories appear to us to be; and his giving them to the world as true has been adduced as a blot on his moral rectitude. But the reader should again be reminded of what has been said in a former page, of the unscientific character of the age he lived in, and of the general atmosphere of thought, especially in monastic circles. The stories that carry with them the most interest are those told of St. Benedict, to whom the second book of the Dialogues is devoted. They help us to a view of the man, of his career and character. One incident told respecting him, and the comment made on it, is peculiarly pleasing. Benedict, though secluded in his monastery, kept a warm heart for his sister, who was a devotee like himself, but who used to come to see him once a year. One year, shortly before her death, she came as usual, and spent the day with him in some building not far from his monastery. As they took their evening meal together, she begged him to stay with her till her departure; but he refused, on the ground of the rule requiring him to spend the night in his cell. Whereupon she bent her head over the table in prayer, and in answer to her prayer such a violent thunderstorm came on as rendered it impossible for her brother to leave her till the morning. Gregory comments thus on the incident, which he calls a miracle:—" I said that there had been one thing which he wished, but could not obtain. Nor is it wonderful that in this case a woman, who desired her brother's presence, prevailed more than he; for, since, according to the words of John, 'God is love,' it was right that she who had the greater love should have the greater power." Peter is made to say, on hearing this: "I confess that what you say pleases me much." And Gregory goes on to tell him that three days after her return to her convent the sister died; that Benedict had a vision of her soul departing in the form of a dove, and had her body brought to his own monastery for burial; "so that they whose souls had always been one in God, even in their burial were not divided."

The fourth book of the Dialogues refers especially to the state of the soul after death. The belief in its survival, notwithstanding its invisibility, is first justified against intellectual difficulties by philosophical arguments, which are forcible and well put, and then supported by a number of stories—revelations to dying persons, visions of the departed to survivors, and experiences of some who had returned to life from apparent death. The eternity of future punishment is maintained, and attempts made to reconcile the conception of it with the Divine attributes. Other difficulties attending the received views about the future state, such as that of a literal fire tormenting disembodied spirits, are also met by arguments. The view of a purgtaorial fire for the imperfectly good is treated as one to be accepted, but not laid down positively, the Romish doctrine of purgatory not having as yet assumed any definite

form. But on this head, as well as with regard to the unseen world in general, there is no doubt that Gregory's Dialogues have gone far to give shape to the mediæval conceptions on such subjects. It will be perceived from the above cursory review, that, in this fourth book at least, the writer appears as a thinker and reasoner, as well as a relater of marvels; and he shows a clear perception of intellectual difficulties and considerable power of argument. Lastly we may adduce, as evidence of his appreciation of the religion of the heart underlying all superstitious views with which he may be charged, the conclusion of the whole treatise; where, after discoursing on and illustrating the salutary effect of the Eucharistic oblation for the dead as well as the living, he adds —" But it is necessary that, when we do these things, we sacrifice ourselves to God in the contrition of the heart; since we who celebrate the mysteries of the Lord's passion ought to imitate what we celebrate. For then will God be truly a sacrifice for us, when we shall have made ourselves a sacrifice." . . .
"Wherefore, while time is still allowed us, while the judge tarries, and waits for our conversion, let us bewail with tears the hardness of our mind, let us form in ourselves the grace of loving-kindness to our neighbours. And I boldly say that we shall not need this salutary host after death, if before death we have been ourselves a host to God."

The longest and most ambitious literary work of Gregory is his commentary on Job, in thirty-five books (known as *Magna Moralia*), begun at Constantinople during his intimacy with Leander of Seville, and finished afterwards, and dedicated to him. Few readers of the present day will have patience enough to wade through this elaborate dissertation, of which the following good account is given by Milman, in his "History of Latin Christianity":—"The book of Job, according to Gregory, comprehended in itself all natural, all Christian, theology, and all morals. It was at once a true and wonderful history, an allegory containing, in its secret sense, the whole theory of the Christian church and Christian sacraments, and a moral philosophy applicable to all mankind. As an interpreter of the history, Gregory was entirely ignorant of all the Oriental languages, even of Greek. He read the book partly according to the older, partly according to the later Latin version. Of ancient or of Oriental manners he knew nothing. Of the book of Job as a poem (the most sublime of all antiquity) he had no conception; to him it is all pure, unimaginative, unembellished history. As an allegory, it is surprising with what copious ingenuity Gregory discovers latent adumbrations of all the Christian doctrines, and still more the unrelenting condemnation of heresies and of heretics. The moral interpretation may be read at the present time, if with no great admiration at the depth of the philosophy, with respect for its loftiness and purity. It is ascetic, but generally, except when heretics are concerned, devout, humane, and generous." The following may serve as a specimen of the allegorical interpretation. On the text, "There were born unto him seven sons and three daughters. His substance also was seven thousand sheep, and three thousand camels, and five hundred yoke of oxen, and five hundred she asses," he comments to this effect. The seven sons mean the twelve apostles, and therefore the clergy, because seven is the perfect number, and multiplied within itself, four by three or three by four, produces twelve. The three daughters mean the faithful laity, because they are to worship the Trinity. The seven thousand sheep mean the multitude of Jewish converts, since they came from the pastures of the law; the three thousand camels the multitude of Gentiles, the camels denoting Gentiles as carrying burdens, for the Gentiles were burdened with their idolatrous superstitions, but laid them down when they came to Christ; and the same thing is shown by Rebecca having ridden on a camel, expressing her Gentile condition, when she journeyed to meet Isaac, but alighted from it when she saw him. Or the camel may denote the Samaritans, inasmuch as it chews the cud, but does not part the hoof; for the Samaritans receive the law in part, but in part reject it. The oxen and asses are explained in a similar style. It may seem surprising that a man of Gregory's mental powers and culture could interpret in this fashion; a fashion which allows anything whatever to be drawn out of the text according to the mind of the interpreter. But he started with the view, not confined to him, that all Scripture, being directly inspired by the Holy Ghost, had a mystic as well as a literal meaning; and the occupation of searching out this meaning seems to have carried him away with a kind of fascination. Further, in justice to him it should be noted that his giving often alternative interpretations implies that he did not set himself up as an infallible exponent of the mystic sense.

Gregory considered preaching an important part of the pastoral office. We find him expressing regret that he had so little time for it. Two collections of his sermons remain, twenty-two homilies on Ezekiel, and forty on the Gospels for the day. The former have been alluded to above as preached for the edification of the people of Rome during the great distress caused by one of the Lombard invasions. They were revised and edited by himself, as he mentions in his letter to a bishop, Marianus, who had asked to see them, eight years after their delivery. They abound in the allegorical interpretations of the text which he was so fond of, and for which the subject chosen gave peculiar scope, but are also didactic and hortatory. The first of them is an exposition of the scope of prophecy generally, which he shows to embrace the past, the present, and the future, rightly taking the word to express a showing forth of hidden things rather than prediction only; and he concludes it thus: "Saying these things, in our preface alone, we here have, as it were, made trial of our ship in harbour, that we may afterwards spread our sails for exploring the mysteries of prophecy, as it were in the immensity of the ocean. Which thing, however, we presume not to do in our own strength, but in Him who has made the tongues of babes eloquent, 'for the spirit of the Lord filleth the world; and that which containeth all things hath knowledge of the voice.' For the voice of the Almighty Father is God Almighty. And desiring to speak of Him, in Him we shall be in no wise mute. For the Almighty Word will give us profitable words; He who, for us incarnate, lives and reigns with the Father in the unity of the Holy Spirit, God for ever and ever. Amen." The homilies on the Gospels were delivered during celebration on various occasions, and afterwards collected by himself. Each of them consists of an exposition in detail of the Gospel that had been read, followed by application and exhortation, often very apt and forcible. Occasionally recent incidents, some of them of a supposed miraculous character, are adduced by way of enforcing his appeal. As a specimen of the hortatory style we may cite the peroration of the last homily in the collection, on the parable of Dives and Lazarus. After expounding it both allegorically and literally, he relates a story (told to him by one who knew) about Romula, a religious woman, who, after a life of holy poverty, and after long suffering from paralysis, had departed among heavenly signs. A few days before her death, a sudden light filled her room, the sound as of a multitude pressing into it had been heard, though no person had been seen, and a sweet odour had been left behind. On the day of her departure, voices as of alternate choirs of males and females had been heard outside her door, which seemed to die away in the distance as her soul took its flight. Having spoken of her as one of God's pearls, lifted from the dunghill of humiliation and corruptibility "to glitter among those unknown stones in the eternal diadem of the heavenly King," he proceeds: "O ye who are rich in this world, or imagine yourselves to be so, compare, if you can, your false riches with the true riches of Romula. You, in your way through this world, possess, but will lose everything; she sought nothing in her journey, but has found everything at its close. You lead a joyful life, but fear a sorrowful death; she endured a sorrowful life, but attained to a joyful death. You for a time seek honour from men; she, despised of men, has found angels as her companions. Learn then, brethren, to despise all temporal things. Learn to contemn transitory honour, to love eternal glory. Honour those whom you see poor, and such as you perceive to be outwardly the despised of the world regard as inwardly the friends of God. Share with them what you have, that they may deign some time to share what they have with you. Consider what is said by the mouth of the teacher of the Gentiles, 'That now at this time your abundance may be a supply for their want, that their abundance also may be a supply for your want.' Consider what the Truth itself says: 'Inasmuch as ye have done it to one of the least of these My brethren, ye have done it unto Me.' Why then are you slow to give, when what you bestow on one lying on the earth you give to one that sits in heaven? But what Almighty God through me speaks in your ears, may He speak Himself in your minds, who liveth and reigneth with the Father, in the unity of the Holy Spirit, God for ever and ever. Amen."

The liturgical works of Gregory are his Sacramentary, his Antiphonary, and certain hymns imputed to him with probability. The Roman Sacramentary in use before his time was that of Pope Gelasius

(492-496), founded on an earlier one compiled by St. Leo (440-461). What Gregory did, according to his biographer, John the Deacon, was to abbreviate the Gelasian codex into the compass of one volume, omitting much, changing a few things, and adding others. These omissions, changes, and additions seem to have been mainly in the variable parts of the service for different days and seasons. In the invariable part—the Ordinarium and Canon— the only changes attributed to him are two in the Canon, which are noticed by Bede; viz., the introduction of the Lord's Prayer immediately after the Consecration, and the addition to the prayer of Oblation of the words, "and dispose our days in Thy peace, and grant us to be rescued from eternal damnation, and numbered in the flock of Thine elect." His introduction of the Lord's Prayer where it still occurs in the Roman "Canon" is alluded to in a letter of his own to John, Bishop of Syracuse, in which he defends this and other changes against some who had taunted him with imitating the use of Constantinople. This, he says, he had not done, inasmuch as in the East the Lord's Prayer was repeated in this place by all the people, but in the Roman Church by the priest alone. And he justifies his introduction of it in the part of the service referred to, by the remarkable assertion (his grounds for which are not known) that the apostles had used no other prayer than the Lord's Prayer in consecrating the elements. His words are, "But we say the Lord's Prayer immediately after the prayer (of consecration), because it was the custom of the apostles to consecrate the host of oblation by that prayer only. And it seemed to me very unsuitable that we should say over the oblation a prayer which some scholastic had composed, and to omit saying that prayer which our Redeemer Himself composed over His Body and Blood."[1] His assertion about the apostles having used the Lord's Prayer only in consecrating the Eucharist has been the subject of considerable discussion. The liturgist Bona thinks it so unlikely to be true, that he suggests that the word "only" (*solum-modo*) has crept into the text, regarding it as incredible that the apostles should not at any rate have recited the words of institution. Binterin suggests "solemni modo" as the true reading for "solum-modo," or that the word "only" refers to the occasion of using the prayer, not to the prayer itself; the meaning being, according to this last view, that the apostles used the Lord's Prayer in the consecration of the Eucharist, but not in the celebration of other sacraments. But all these are only lame devices for getting out of a supposed difficulty. Daniel (*Codex Liturgicus*) sees no difficulty in the assertion. He takes Gregory to be referring to that part of the office only which is still called "the Consecration," beginning with "Who on the day before He suffered"; and considers him to mean, that in this particular part the apostles added no prayer but the Lord's Prayer to the words of Institution, which he never thought of denying their use of. The form of prayer which follows the words

[1] Epp., B. VII., Ind. ii., Ep. 64.

of Institution in the Roman use he supposes to have been subsequently composed by some one known as "Scholasticus." According to this theory, Gregory's words do not imply that the Apostles used no prayers but the Lord's Prayer in the celebration of the Eucharist previously or subsequently to the actual consecration of the elements, only that the consecration prayer of the Roman Canon, and of other ancient liturgies, was not apostolic. The further apparent inference from the words of both Bede and Gregory himself, that the Lord's Prayer did not occur at all in the Roman office before his time, has also been a source of difficulty. Muratori scouts the idea that the inference can be a correct one. Bona acknowledges that it is the natural one from the words used, and supposes that though it had originally been in the Roman as in other ancient offices, the custom may have crept in of omitting it; adducing in illustration a similar custom in the Church of Spain about the same period: "Some priests in Spain are found who say the Lord's Prayer which our Saviour taught and commanded, not daily, but on the Lord's day only."[1] He also suggests the view, which is now generally taken, that all that Gregory did was to remove the Lord's Prayer to its present place immediately after consecration, from some other part of the office where it had previously occurred, either before or afterwards. And what Gregory says is quite compatible with this view. It is sometimes taken almost

---

[1] Concil. Toleton., iv. 9.

for granted that it had previously occurred after the fraction of the host, and before communion, as in most other ancient liturgies. But Gregory's words, "over His Body and Blood," seem to preclude its previous use at all between consecration and communion. Hence, if we suppose it to have occurred in some other part of the office, either before or afterwards, it would appear that the reformed Anglican office agrees in this respect with the Roman use before the time of Gregory. It follows also that the ancient Roman liturgy differed in the same respect from all ancient ones that we know of, except indeed the "Clementine" (considered to be the earliest type of Eucharistic service), in which the Lord's Prayer does not occur at all. There seems to be no doubt that the "Ordo Missæ," exclusive of the parts which vary with the seasons, has remained unaltered since his time, though it is uncertain how much of the rest is of later introduction. Similar uncertainty rests on the Antiphonary, or book of Antiphons, that bears his name. Among the hymns that have been attributed to him, many are undoubtedly of a later date. The Benedictine editors of his works have selected eight as his, as they probably may be. Their versification on the whole seems to be such as to suit his age, being in the main classical, though not strictly so. Six of them are in the metre generally used by St. Ambrose, viz., strophes of four lines of Iambic dimeters, corresponding to the long measure of our English hymns: two are in what is called Sapphic verse. Most of them are without rhyme, though in some it occurs occasionally, possibly without deliberate intention. One only (that on the Passion, beginning "Rex Christe, factor omnium") is in rhyme throughout. This circumstance, joined with the fact that the earliest manuscript copies of it are as late as the 12th century, suggests the suspicion that it (as well as the verses of the other hymns where rhymes occur) may be by some later hand. But, if rhymed verses were beginning to come into use in Gregory's age, it is quite supposable that he might write in both styles. The rhymed hymn just alluded to is interesting, as being spoken of by Luther in his Table-talk as the best ever written. The devotional tone of these hymns is not, like that of many later ones, individually subjective; being such as rather to suit a community of worshippers, and with references to the acts of creation and redemption, and to the life of Christ. We may suppose them to have been especially intended for use in monasteries. They include well-known favourites of our day, whether used in Latin or in translations. Many will recognize them by their initial lines, which are,—1. *Primo dierum omnium;* 2. *Nocte surgentes vigilemus omnes;* 3. *Ecce jam noctis tenuatur umbra;* 4. *Lucis Creator optime;* 5. *Clarum decus jejunii;* 6. *Audi beate Conditor;* 7. *Magno salutis gaudio;* 8. *Rex Christe factor omnium.*

It may be added, for the sake of those who cannot refer to the originals, that of these Nos. 4, 5, and 6 appear, translated or paraphrased, in "Hymns Ancient and Modern," under the titles, "Blest Creator of the light," "Good it is to keep the fast," and "O Merciful Creator, hear."

He took great interest in ritual,—whence he has

been called "Master of Ceremonies" (*Magister cærimoniorum*), and, in connection with it, in church music. He founded a song-school at Rome, which had also a charitable purpose, being called "The Orphanage" (*Orphanotrophium*), with two buildings, one beneath the steps leading to St. Peter's Church, the other adjoining the Lateran palace; and there it was that he personally instructed the boys in music. We all know something of the "Gregorian tones," so called from him, which, at any rate, represent the kind of music he promoted. He is said to have banished all that was light and theatrical from church music, and also to have confined the singing to the choir, excluding the general congregation. The preference thus shown for the ancient and severe style, due we may suppose to his monastic predilections, is probably what gave the distinguishing character to what used to be called "Gregorian" as opposed to "Ambrosian" music. For the terms "Cantus Gregorianus" and "Cantus Ambrosianus" we find used formerly as marking two distinct styles. Now what we know positively of the kind of singing favoured by St. Ambrose is this. He introduced in his church at Milan the antiphonal chanting, which had spread from Antioch through the East before it found its way into the West;[1] and also, it appears, such a peculiarly pleasing and melodious style of music that St. Augustine, when he first heard it, doubted its propriety, though it charmed him. He

---

[1] Theodoret, ii. 24; Socrates, vi. 8; Nicetas, "*Thesaur. Orthodox. Fid.*," v. 30; Augustine, "*Confess.*," ix. 7; Paulinus, *in Vit. Ambrosii.*

says with reference to it, addressing Ambrose, "But, when I remember my tears which I shed on hearing the singing in your church, in the beginning of my recovered faith, and how I am now also moved by it, not by the singing itself, but by that which is sung with liquid voice and most suitable modulation, I again acknowledge the great utility of this system. And thus I fluctuate between a feeling of danger from the pleasure it gives and experience of its advantage; and I am on the whole inclined (though not giving a settled opinion) to approve your way of singing in church, that, through the ear's delight the mind may be roused to pious emotions." It would seem that before St. Ambrose gave his sanction to melodious and attractive music, the heretics had been allowed to monopolize it. At any rate, at Alexandria (as St. Augustine also informs us) St. Athanasius had instructed the readers of the Psalms to use such moderate inflections of the voice that it was more like recitation than singing; and the African Donatists reproached the Catholics for the dulness of their psalmody. It was probably an analogous case to that of old-fashioned Church of England people regarding at first with suspicion and dislike the exciting hymnody of Methodists. Thus we have good reason to suppose the style of music called Ambrosian to have been, in its essence, that of attractive melody, which may have developed into fantastic lightness in the time of Gregory. And it is probable that Gregory's reform was a return, in some degree, to the more severe ancient style, and that this was the real difference in principle between

Ambrosian and Gregorian music. This view is confirmed by what we are told, as above stated, of Gregory having banished all that was light and theatrical from the music of the Church, and also by the statement of an ancient writer (quoted by the liturgist Martene[1]) that in the Benedictine monastery of Cassino Ambrosian music was entirely forbidden to be sung. It has been commonly alleged that Gregory's main work in regard to church music was an extension of the modes or scales previously in use; that Ambrose, having introduced the four "authentic" modes called (after those in ancient Greek music that corresponded with them) Dorian, Phrygian, Lydian, Misco-Lydian, Gregory added to them the four "plagal" or "subsidiary" modes, called Hypo-Dorian, Hypo-Phrygian, Hypo-Lydian, Hypo-Misco-Lydian, thus enlarging the range of allowed ecclesiastical melody. But, whatever ground there may be for this statement, it evidently does not account for the contrast anciently made between Ambrosian and Gregorian music; and Mr. Chappell, in his recently published *History of Music*, maintains that the ecclesiastical scales referred to "are not of the early date that has been supposed."

---

[1] Martene, "*De Antiq. Eccles. Rit.*," vol. iii. p. 8.

CHAPTER VIII.

Gregory's Character—His talents—His attainments—His doctrinal views—On the authority of the Church—Augustinianism—Baptism—The Eucharist—Purgatory—Intercession of Saints—Relics—Pictures and Images—Slavery—Authority of the Roman See—Results of his policy.

OF the character, the talents, and the attainments of Pope Gregory the reader will, it is hoped, have gained a pretty clear conception from the acts of his life, and especially from the extracts that have been given from his letters and other writings. Of the loftiness of his aims, the earnestness of his purpose, the fervour of his devotion, his unwearied activity, and his personal purity, there can be no doubt. These qualities are conspicuous through his whole career. If his religion was of the strongly ascetic type, and disfigured by superstitious credulity, it bore in these respects the complexion of his age, inseparable then from aspiration after the highest holiness. Nor did either superstition or asceticism supersede in him the principles of a true inward religion,—justice, mercy, and truth. We find him, when occasion required, exalting mercy above sacrifice; he was singularly kindly and benevolent, as well as just; and even his zeal for the full rigour of monastic discipline was tempered with much gentleness and allowance for infirmity. If, again, with singleness of main purpose was combined at times the astuteness of the diplomatist, and a certain degree of politic insincerity in addressing potentates, his aims were never personal or selfish. And if he could stoop, for the attainment of his ends, to the then prevalent adulation of the great, he could also speak his mind fearlessly to the greatest, when he felt great principles to be at stake.

His talents were eminently of the practical order; such as enabled him at once to organize large plans, and to direct the details of their execution; to keep in his own hands the reins of a multitude of affairs, and make himself felt in remote regions. He had the rare gift of uniting zeal with prudence; he was singularly free from stiffness and prejudice in adapting his course to circumstances, though without losing sight of the end in view: he could pursue a wise policy of accommodation without sacrifice of principle. He had eminently the gifts of government and administration. He had moreover the power of gaining influence over other minds, with the important gift of tact in his mode of addressing various people. In the higher intellectual sphere he was not much of an original thinker or a philosopher; but he could see clearly and grasp firmly the tenets of orthodox theology, and expound them to others, generally with a practical purpose. He was altogether a practical rather than a theoretical theologian. His attainments also were limited. Though spoken of in his youth as second to none in Rome in grammar, logic, and rhetoric, which constituted then a liberal education, and though he had further studied Roman law, and was thoroughly familiar with Holy Scripture, yet he knew no language but his own, was unacquainted with classical literature, and showed himself utterly incompetent as a critical expositor of the Bible. As to the classics, he avoided them on principle, as being heathen. There is indeed no good ground for crediting the story (the earliest authority for which is John of Salisbury in the 12th century) of his having purposely burnt the Palatine library; but his feelings with regard to heathen literature sufficiently appear from his letter of strong reproof to Desiderius, bishop of Vienne, for giving lessons in grammar, on the ground that the occupation involved the reading of heathen poets. "For (says he) the praises of Christ do not admit of being joined in the same mouth with the praises of Jupiter; and it is a serious and execrable thing for bishops to sing what even for a religious layman is unbecoming."[1] Thus the fancy, the grace, the thoughts, of the master minds of antiquity; ancient history and philosophy; those things which we now regard as the means of the highest intellectual culture; were precluded by his very principles from shedding their light upon his mind: even the old Christian fathers he does not seem to have studied deeply, though he was familiar with St. Augustine, and had imbibed his views: the very Bible he knew only through Latin translations; and though he thus knew it intimately, and had it, as it were, at his fingers' ends, and understood well its moral and religious teaching, he had little collateral knowledge or

---

[1] Ep., B. IX., Ind. iv., Ep. 48.

enlightenment to enable him to interpret it with intelligent breadth of view. He represented and perpetuated the domination of received theological conceptions over all fields of thought which had already set in, and which continued through the middle ages, till the Renaissance gave men's minds a freer wing. Still, within the range he took, he spoke to his own and succeeding ages with great power and influence; while his genuine piety and his real grasp of essential Christian principles enabled him so to speak as to justify his title as a doctor of the Church.

A short notice of the doctrinal views prominent in his works shall be given in conclusion; being interesting as showing both the beliefs of his day, and the action of his own mind upon them.

The dogmatic decisions of the general councils with respect to the Trinity and the Incarnation he accepted implicitly, though the constitution and bent of his mind were not such as to lead him to dwell in his writings on the abstruse subjects involved. What the Church Catholic had authoritatively ruled he regarded as settled, and beyond the range of dispute. And the Church he compares to the ark of Noah, within which alone was salvation, and with four sides to it, which denote the four Gospels, the four œcumenical Councils, and the four Patriarchates. Within these four sides, thus variously understood, was both truth and salvation. On the doctrines of Grace he adopted the teaching of his favourite divine, St. Augustine, referring the salvation of individuals entirely to divine election, though he is careful to recognize the operation of human freewill as the organ through which grace works. "The good which we do is both God's and ours: God's, through prevenient grace; ours, through freewill complying."[1] "Since, when divine grace prevents us, our freewill follows, we are said to make ourselves free, in consenting to the Lord, who makes us free."[2] But all is ultimately referred to the eternal knowledge of God, which is regarded as causal, as well as infinite. "We know that to God nothing is future; before His eyes there is no past, present things pass not away, future things come not: since everything which to us was and will be in His sight is present; and whatever is present He may be said to know rather than foreknow. Because He sees things which to us are future, but to Himself are always present, He is said to be prescient; although He by no means foresees as future what He sees as present; for whatever is is not seen in His eternity because it is, but is because it is seen."[3] Gregory was thus influential in handing on to the Church the Augustinian theology; but in its milder and more practical, rather than its speculative form. He mainly concerned himself with that side of it which he held conducive to the formation of the Christian character, to humility, and dependence on God. Speculative difficulties on this and other abstruse subjects he was by no means blind to; but met them by reference to the inscrutability of the

---

[1] "Commentary on Job," book xxxiii. in ch. 41.
[2] Ibid., book xxiv. in ch. 33.
[3] Ibid., book xx. in ch. 30.

divine counsels. He reproved heretics for their tendency to investigate, instead of accepting, the secrets of God, so that, "aiming at knowledge of the divine nature, they remained ignorant of themselves." In this tone of feeling (as has appeared from one of his quoted letters) he esteemed it neither possible, nor profitable if it were so, to be assured in this life of one's own election. Following the same line of thought, he ends one of his sermons thus: "Let us trust in the mercy of our Creator: let us, being mindful of His righteousness, lament our sins; being mindful of His grace, let us not despair. The Godman gives man trust in God." Similarly the then received view of unbaptized infants being rejected while the baptized were saved, the difficulty of which he sees, he declines to discuss, on the ground of the whole subject being obscure, and beyond human comprehension.

His general view of the Sacrament of Baptism is set forth in a letter to Theoctista, which has been already referred to and quoted. He regards it as entirely cleansing the recipient from the guilt of all past sin, starting him on a new life of theoretic holiness; but by no means securing him against new temptations, which may frustrate his attainment of salvation. "If there are any that say that sins are only superficially remitted in baptism, what can be more unbelieving than such teaching, by which the very sacrament of faith is nullified? In it especially the soul is bound to the mystery of celestial purity, that, being entirely absolved from all sins, it may cleave to Him alone, of whom the prophet says, 'It is good for me to hold me fast by God.' For certainly the passage of the Red Sea was a figure of holy baptism, in which the enemies behind died, but others in front were found in the wilderness. In like manner, all who are washed in holy baptism have all their past sins remitted, since they die as the Egyptian did. But in the wilderness we find other enemies; since, as long as we live in this life, ere we attain to the country of promise, many temptations assail us, and stand in the way of those who are travelling to the land of the living."[1]

He took a high and mystic view of the Eucharistic sacrifice, though without any definite explanation of the mode of Christ's presence. The particular theory of transubstantiation had not then been mooted. He writes of the Eucharist thus: "For this sacrifice in a peculiar manner saves the soul from eternal death, renewing to us through a mystery that death of the Only-begotten, who, though being risen from the dead He dieth no more, and death shall have no more dominion over Him, yet, while in Himself living immortally and incorruptibly, is again sacrificed for us in this mystery of the sacred oblation. For His body is there taken, His flesh is distributed for the salvation of the people, His blood is shed, not into the hands of unbelievers, but into the mouths of the faithful. Ponder we then of what sort to us is this sacrifice, which for our absolution ever imitates the passion of the only-begotten Son. For who of the faithful can doubt that, in the very hour

[1] B. XI., Ind. iv., Ep. 45.

of immolation, at the priest's voice the heavens are opened; that in this mystery of Jesus Christ the choirs of angels are present, the lowest is associated with the highest, things on earth are joined to things in heaven, the visible and invisible become one?"[1] He believed also in its efficacy, when offered with a special intention, for the benefit of absent persons, causing sometimes their sudden delivery from temporal calamities, and for the absolution of departed souls in pain. Several stories are told in his "Dialogues" illustrative of such results. But, on the other hand, we must not forget his view, expressed in a passage that has been quoted, of the sacrifice not benefiting the worshippers unless they imitate what they celebrate by a moral sacrifice of themselves, and of their needing no other after death, if during life they have offered this.

His belief in a purgatorial fire of some kind has been already referred to: which belief, though not propounded in the way of positive dogma, yet, supported as it was by stories, attested by visions, of the efficacy of masses for souls in pain, is believed to have formed an important step towards the formation of the later more definite doctrine on the subject. His favourite theologian, St. Augustine, had spoken of the belief of some in a cleansing fire after death, which he regards as not improbable. Gregory advances the theory more positively, as what " is to be believed." He grounds the view mainly on the reason of the case rather than on distinct revelation, arguing that, as no

[1] Dial. IV. 58.

unclean thing can enter heaven, and as many depart this life who seem neither good enough for heaven nor bad enough for hell, there must surely be a purgatory. But he also cites 1 Cor. iii. 12 in support of his position. It is almost needless to say that the Romish theory of papal indulgences, as applied to souls in purgatory, was in his time unknown.

The saint-worship, and especially the Mariolatry of a later age, derive no sanction from the writings of Gregory, except so far as their germs may be found in the long-standing belief in the value of the intercession of beatified saints, to which he gives expression. He speaks, especially in letters when he asserts the authority of the Roman see, of the value of St. Peter's mediation for obtaining remission of sin. But there is a marked distinction between his utterances on the subject and the subsequently developed *cultus* of saints, and especially of the Blessed Virgin. And in his Sacramentary the prayers where the intercession of saints is pleaded are addressed to God, not to the saints themselves.

In the efficacy of relics he fully believed; sent presents of them to distinguished converts and other devout persons; ordered their deposition in newly-founded churches; and recognized miracles wrought by their means.

His views on the subject appear strikingly in a letter to the Empress Constantina, who had asked him for the head of St. Paul, or something from his body, that she might place it in a church which she had built in honour of the Apostle. He tells her that he neither could nor dared comply with her request, for that the bodies of St. Peter and St. Paul at Rome were surrounded by such miracles and terrors that they could not be approached, even for the purpose of prayer, without great fear. Pope Leo, he says, had once desired to change some silver in the shrine of St. Peter, at a distance of fifteen paces from the body itself, but had been deterred by a terrible sign. He himself had been similarly deterred from altering something near the body of St. Paul, and a person who had presumed to lift and remove some bones in the neighbourhood, but not in the grave itself, had seen awful portents, and died suddenly. Further, in the time of Pope Leo, the body of St. Laurentius having, in the course of some alterations, been accidentally exposed, all who were present and saw it, though they had not presumed to touch it, had died within ten days.

He adds that it was the custom at Rome never to allow relics from the bodies of saints to be carried away, but only to place near them pieces of cloth enclosed in a box, which, when afterwards deposited in newly-dedicated churches, were found to possess the same miraculous powers as the bodies themselves. The genuineness of one such cloth had been questioned by some Greeks in the days of Leo, who had thereupon cut it with a pair of scissors, and blood had flowed from it.

As to the bodies of saints, it was held throughout the West to be altogether intolerable and sacrilegious to touch them. It was asserted, indeed, that in the East it was customary to remove their bones; but this Gregory can hardly believe, and he is confirmed in his opinion by the fact that certain Greeks had recently been found digging by night near St. Paul's church at Rome, and had confessed, on being examined, that they were taking away fictitious relics, to be passed off in the East as the real bones of saints.[1]

The controversy about the use and adoration of pictures and images, which ere long gave rise to such bitter conflict, had not yet begun. But there were already signs of its approach; and Gregory, like his successors, defended their use, though he was careful to repudiate any superstitious adoration of them. Serenus, bishop of Marseilles, had, in his zeal against incipient idolatry, destroyed the images in a church. To him Gregory wrote as follows: "We have been informed that, inflamed by inconsiderate zeal, you have broken the images of the saints, on the pretext that they ought not to be adored. And indeed we altogether praise you for forbidding them to be adored, but we blame you for breaking them. Say, brother, what priest has ever been heard to have done what you have done? Ought not this consideration to have checked you, and kept you from despising your brethren, and setting yourself up as the only one that is holy and wise? For it is one thing to adore a picture; another to learn what it is to be adored through the history told by the picture. What Scripture presents to readers, a picture presents to the gaze of the unlearned: for in it even the ignorant see what they ought to follow;

[1] B. IV., Ind. xii., Ep. 30.

in it the illiterate read."[1] In a letter also to one Secundinus, who was not an illiterate person, he says,

"The images which you asked for I have sent. Your request for them has pleased me much, since with all your heart you seek Him whose image you desire to have before your eyes. We do nothing unreasonable if by the visible we show forth the invisible. Thus a man ardently desirous of seeing another,—say a lover anxious to behold his betrothed bride, if she should happen to be going to the bath or to the church,— hastens to meet her on the way, that he may return gladdened by the sight of her. I know that you do not desire the image of our Saviour that you may worship it as God, but that you may be reminded of Him, and refresh your love for Him by the sight of His image. . . . Wherefore we send you images of God the Saviour, of the holy Mary mother of God, and of the apostles Peter and Paul."[2]

His views on slavery, though not, strictly speaking, to be classed among his theological tenets, may be mentioned here. Like St. Paul, he recognized the institution as part of the social system of his day, and respected the rights of masters. He directed slaves to be employed in the service of monasteries, as well as on the lands of the Patrimony, and caused them to be purchased for these purposes. He forbade in synod unrestricted allowance of slaves eluding their

---

[1] B. IX., Ind. iv., Ep. 9.
[2] Epp., B. VII., Ind. ii., Ep. 54.

service on the plea of entering monasteries. But he encouraged their conversion to monastic life, when their sincerity had been proved by probation, at the same time directing, when necessary, their owners to be repaid in money for their loss. He was also zealous in the redemption of captives out of his own means and those of others, and out of general church funds.

In one case we find him freely manumitting two slaves of the Roman Church, and securing to them and their lawful issue in perpetuity certain money that had been left them. His letter on this occasion expresses well his views on slavery in the abstract, and the motives that actuated him. He writes,

"Since our Redeemer, the Maker of every creature, was pleased mercifully to assume human flesh in order to break the chain of slavery in which we were held captive, and restore us to our pristine liberty, it is right that men, whom nature from the beginning produced free, and whom the law of nations has subjected to the yoke of slavery, should be restored by the benefit of manumission to the liberty in which they were born. Wherefore, moved by this consideration, we make you, Montana and Thomas, from this day forth free and Roman citizens, and give you free use of all your private property."[1]

It remains to notice once more Gregory's undoubted view of the universal supremacy of the See of Rome

[1] B. VI., Ind. xiv., Ep. 12.

in virtue of the special commission to St. Peter (called the Prince of the Apostles) by our Lord Himself. But we do not find him asserting it in such a way as to merge the general episcopal commission in the Papacy; to make the Pope the necessary source of all ecclesiastical jurisdiction, or the sole infallible definer of doctrine. His protest against the title assumed by the Constantinopolitan patriarchs has indeed been often rightly quoted as a virtual protest also against many subsequent papal claims. And his remarkable view of Antioch and Alexandria being co-ordinate successors of St. Peter with himself, must also be borne in mind. Still less did he think of asserting the theory of the subjection of the temporal to the spiritual sword, carrying with it the power of setting up or deposing princes, which was afterwards developed, and which was so emphatically expressed in the famous Bull of Boniface VIII. (A.D. 1303), called "Unam Sanctam." On the contrary, he was remarkable, as has been seen, for his deference to the civil power, and his recognition of its supremacy in its proper sphere.

Homage to himself personally as Pope he earnestly repudiated. He discouraged the custom of bishops resorting to Rome, in order to render honour to him, on the anniversaries of his consecration, and in a synod he forbade the dead bodies of popes, when carried to burial, to be covered with a dalmatic, lest the people (as they had been accustomed to do) should tear off pieces of it as sacred relics: for, he said, bishops of Rome are sinners like other men. Still, there can be no doubt that it was eminently his astute and comprehensive policy that brought about the system of papal monarchy which, though ever repudiated in the East, was finally accepted by the whole of the Western Church. Without inquiring here into the soundness of the theory on which it was made to rest, or the evils attending its later development, we may all acknowledge its advantages, or even necessity, in the times for which it was providentially ordained. Christendom indeed owes a deep debt of gratitude to Gregory for this most important issue of his reign. On this head the wise remarks of Milman, in his "History of Latin Christianity," may be suitably quoted in conclusion. "Providence might have otherwise ordained, but it is impossible for man to imagine by what other organizing or consolidating force the commonwealth of the Western nations could have grown up into a discordant, indeed, and conflicting league, but still to a league, with that unity and conformity of manners, usages, laws, religion, which have made their rivalries, oppugnancies, and even their long ceaseless wars, on the whole to issue in the noblest, highest, most intellectual form of civilization known to man. It is inconceivable that Teutonic Europe, or Europe so deeply impregnated with Teutonism, could have been condensed or compelled into a vast Asiatic despotism, or succession of despotisms. Immense and interminable as have been the evils and miseries of the conflict between the southern and northern, the Teutonic and Roman, the hierarchical and civil elements of our social system ; yet out of these conflicts have at length arisen the balance and harmony of the great states which constitute European Christendom, and are now peopling other continents with kindred and derivative institutions. It is impossible to conceive what had been the confusion, the lawlessness, the chaotic state of the middle ages, without the medieval Papacy,—and of the medieval Papacy the real father is Gregory the Great."

CHRONOLOGICAL TABLE OF THE PRINCIPAL EVENTS REFERRED TO.

A.D.
- 404. Seat of Western Empire removed to Revenna.
- 410. Capture of Rome by Alaric.
- 431. Council of Ephesus.
- 451. Council of Chalcedon.
- 452. Invasion of Italy by Attila.
- 455. Capture of Rome by Genseric.
- 461. Death of Pope Leo.
- 476. Odoacer becomes King of Italy.
- 493. Accession of Theodoric.
- 496. Conversion of Clovis.
- 529. Foundation of Monastery of Monte Cassino.
- 536. Reconquest of Italy by Belisarius.
- 540. (?) Birth of Gregory.
- 544. Condemnation of the Three Chapters by Justinian.
- 553. Fifth Œcumenical Council.
- 568. Conquest of Northern Italy by the Lombards.
- 578. Accession of Pope Pelagius.
- 582. Accession of the Emperor Mauricius.
- 589. Council of Toledo.   Reccared embraces Catholicity.
- 590. Gregory elected Pope.
- 591. He summons the Istrian Bishops to Rome.
- ,, Commences measures against the Donatists.
- 592. Writes to the Irish Bishops.
- ,, Hadrianus of Thebes appeals to Gregory.
- 593. Edict of Mauricius about Soldiers becoming Monks.
- ,, Election of Maximus to the See of Salona.
- ,, Gregory remonstrates with John the Faster about the two priests.
- 594. Agilulph invades the Exarchate.
- 595. Truce effected with the Lombards.
- ,, Gregory protests against the the title of Universal Bishop.
- ,, Childebert requests the Pall for Virgilius of Arles.
- 596. Agilulph again invades the Exarchate.
- ,, Death of John the Faster.   Cyriacus succeeds him.
- ,, Mission of Augustine to England.
- 597. Baptism of Ethelbert.
- 599. Conversion of Agilulph to Catholicity.
- 601. Accession of Phocas.
- 606. Death of Gregory.

WYMAN AND SONS, PRINTERS,
GREAT QUEEN STREET, LINCOLN'S INN FIELDS,
LONDON, W.C.

PUBLICATIONS
OF THE
Society for Promoting Christian Knowledge.

THE
FATHERS FOR ENGLISH READERS.

A Series of Monographs on the Chief Fathers of the Church, the Fathers selected being centres of influence at important periods of Church History and in important spheres of action.

Fcap. 8vo., cloth boards, 2s. each.

LEO THE GREAT.
By the Rev. CHARLES GORE, M.A.

GREGORY THE GREAT.
By the Rev. J. BARMBY, B.D.

SAINT AMBROSE: his Life, Times, and Teaching.
By the Rev. ROBINSON THORNTON, D.D.

SAINT AUGUSTINE.
By the Rev. E. L. CUTTS, B.A.

SAINT BASIL THE GREAT.
By the Rev. RICHARD T. SMITH, B.D.

SAINT HILARY OF POITIERS, AND SAINT MARTIN OF TOURS.
By the Rev. J. GIBSON CAZENOVE, D.D.

SAINT JEROME.
By the Rev. EDWARD L. CUTTS, B.A.

SAINT JOHN OF DAMASCUS.
By the Rev. J. H. LUPTON, M.A.

SYNESIUS OF CYRENE, Philosopher and Bishop.
By ALICE GARDNER.

THE APOSTOLIC FATHERS.
By the Rev. H. S. HOLLAND.

THE DEFENDERS OF THE FAITH; or, The Christian Apologists of the Second and Third Centuries.
By the Rev. F. WATSON, M.A.

THE VENERABLE BEDE.
By the Rev. G. F. BROWNE.

PUBLICATIONS OF THE SOCIETY

NON-CHRISTIAN RELIGIOUS SYSTEMS.

A Series of Manuals which furnish in a brief and popular form an accurate account of the great Non-Christian Religious Systems of the World.

Fcap. 8vo., cloth boards, 2s. 6d. each.

Buddhism—Being a Sketch of the Life and Teachings of Guatama, the Buddha.
By T. W. RHYS DAVIDS. With Map.

Buddhism in China.
By the Rev. S. BEAL. With Map.

Confucianism and Taouism.
By Professor ROBERT K. DOUGLAS, of the British Museum. With Map.

Hinduism.
By Professor MONIER WILLIAMS. With Map.

Islam and its Founder.
By J. W. H. STOBART. With Map.

The Corân—Its Composition and Teaching, and the Testimony it bears to the Holy Scriptures.
By Sir WILLIAM MUIR, K.C.S.I.

THE HEATHEN WORLD AND ST. PAUL.

This Series is intended to throw light upon the Writings and Labours of the Apostle of the Gentiles.

Fcap. 8vo., cloth boards, 2s. each.

St. Paul in Greece.
By the Rev. G. S. DAVIES. With Map.

St. Paul in Damascus and Arabia.
By the Rev. GEORGE RAWLINSON, M.A., Canon of Canterbury. With Map.

St. Paul at Rome.
By the Very Rev. CHARLES MERIVALE, D.D., D.C.L., Dean of Ely. With Map.

St. Paul in Asia Minor and at the Syrian Antioch.
By the Rev. E. H. PLUMPTRE, D.D. With Map.

FOR PROMOTING CHRISTIAN KNOWLEDGE.

THE HOME LIBRARY.

A Series of Books illustrative of Church History, &c., specially, but not exclusively, adapted for Sunday Reading.

Crown 8vo., cloth boards, 3s. 6d. each.

Black and White. Mission Stories.
   By H. FORDE.

Charlemagne.
   By the Rev. E. L. CUTTS, B.A. With Map.

Constantine the Great: The Union of Church and State.
   By the Rev. EDWARD L. CUTTS.

Great English Churchmen; or, Famous Names in English Church History and Literature.
   By W. H. DAVENPORT ADAMS.

John Hus. The Commencement of Resistance to Papal Authority on the part of the Inferior Clergy.
   By the Rev. A. H. WRATISLAW.

Judæa and her Rulers, from Nebuchadnezzar to Vespasian.
   By M. BRAMSTON. With Map.

Mazarin.
   By GUSTAVE MASSON, Esq.

Military Religious Orders of the Middle Ages: the Hospitallers, the Templars, the Teutonic Knights, and others.
   By the Rev. E. C. WOODHOUSE.

Mitslav; or, the Conversion of Pomerania.
   By the late Right Rev. R. MILMAN, D.D.

Narcissus: A Tale of Early Christian Times.
   By the Right Rev. W. BOYD CARPENTER.

Richelieu.
   By GUSTAVE MASSON, Esq.

Sketches of the Women of Christendom.
   By the Author of "The Chronicles of the Schönberg-Cotta Family."

The Churchman's Life of Wesley.
   By R. DENNY URLIN, Esq.

The Church in Roman Gaul.
   By the Rev. R. T. SMITH. With Map.

The House of God the Home of Man.
   By the Rev. Canon JELF.

The Inner Life, as Revealed in the Correspondence of Celebrated Christians.
   Edited by the Rev. T. ERSKINE.

The Life of the Soul in the World: Its Nature, Needs, Dangers, Sorrows, Aids, and Joys.
   By the Rev. F. C. WOODHOUSE.

The North African Church.
   By the Rev. J. LLOYD. With Map.

Thoughts and Characters; being Selections from the Writings of the Author of "The Chronicles of the Schönberg-Cotta Family."

PUBLICATIONS OF THE SOCIETY.

CONVERSION OF THE WEST.

A Series of Volumes showing how the Conversion of the Chief Races of the West was brought about, and their condition before this occurred.

Fcap. 8vo., cloth boards, 2s. each.

The Celts.
  By the Rev. G. F. MACLEAR, D.D. With Two Maps.

The English.
  By the above Author. With Two Maps.

The Northmen.
  By the above Author. With Map.

The Slavs.
  By the above Author. With Map.

The Continental Teutons.
  By the Very Rev. Dean MERIVALE. With Map.

ANCIENT HISTORY FROM THE MONUMENTS.

This Series of Books is chiefly intended to illustrate the Sacred Scriptures by the results of recent Monumental Researches in the East.

Fcap. 8vo., cloth boards, 2s. each.

Assyria, from the Earliest Times to the Fall of Nineveh.
  By the late GEORGE SMITH, Esq., of the British Museum.

Sinai: from the Fourth Egyptian Dynasty to the Present Day.
  By HENRY S. PALMER, Major R.E., F.R.A.S. With Map.

Babylonia (The History of).
  By the late GEORGE SMITH, Esq. Edited by the Rev. A. H. SAYCE.

Greek Cities and Islands of Asia Minor.
  By the late W. S. W. VAUX, M.A.

Egypt, from the Earliest Times to B.C. 300.
  By the late S. BIRCH, LL.D.

Persia, from the Earliest Period to the Arab Conquest.
  By the late W. S. W. VAUX, M.A.

DEPOSITORIES:
NORTHUMBERLAND AVENUE, CHARING CROSS, W.C.;
43, QUEEN VICTORIA STREET, E.C.; 26, ST. GEORGE'S PLACE, S.W.
BRIGHTON: 135, NORTH STREET.

www.ingramcontent.com/pod-product-compliance
Lightning Source LLC
Chambersburg PA
CBHW020900230426
43666CB00008B/1256